THE MANKIND CREATURE

THE MANKIND CREATURE

BY

Alfred T Pyles

*Sula Too Publishing * Tampa, Florida * 2024*

ISBN: 979-8-9889305-5-6 Paperback

Printed in the United States of America
For information about this title or to order books and/or electronic media, con-
tact the publisher: Sula Too Publishing

www.sulatoo.com/publishing

CONTENTS

Synopsis-There is a Problem

What solutions can we find to address racial disharmony between White and Black Americans? Both sides are constantly talking about this issue, 7 days a week, 365 days a year. However, neither side seems to be willing to take the steps necessary to fix it. Our relationship is like a bad, abusive marriage. When someone is in a bad relationship, the rational thing to do is to leave before someone gets hurt.

Neither Black nor White Americans want to see their loved ones get hurt, emotionally or physically. The relationship between Black and White Americans in America today has always been unlawful, and it continues to be so. It's like a shotgun wedding, where one party was forced into it against their will.

In my writings, I provide an ***analysis of the character of both races, my dreams for the future, and my suggested solutions*** to the ongoing saga of racism in America.

I am exercising my First Amendment right to freedom of speech. I make no apologies for my words. If they offend you, then you must be the one who fits the shoes that my words describe.

Like them, or not.
Agree with them, or not.
I have spoken …

Liberation Proclamation

To ALL of man and mankind, this essay stems from a common man's, grassroot perspective.

Analysis

Many of us have carved out a living speaking on the ills of racist America. The life and death question I ask all American citizens is: **What are our collective solutions** concerning the ongoing saga of race relations among the black, brown, and melanated people in America and Europe?

This solution-focused question is relatively simple, yet it appears to be the ultimate question that modern-day people on both sides seemingly avoid. Both sides have known of the problems for centuries. I should say that black and brown people are aware of what I write since Europeans seem clueless that a problem exists. They don't appear to know about the combustible, explosive element lurking among American citizens waiting for the proper flashpoint. Ignition can and will destroy America's civilization as we know it, at least to some extent.

Some white liberals, numerous black freedom fighters, revolutionaries, and visionaries, past and present, have exposed and expounded upon, the existing crisis. They have offered their perceived solutions to all of America, which has obviously fallen on deaf ears on both sides of the aisle.

Notable black and brown spirits I've gravitated to are Marcus Garvey, John Henrik Clarke, Malcolm X, the Black Panther party, Dr. Frances Cress Welsing, Prof. James Smalls, Dr. Ray Hagins, and Dr. Claud Anderson.

There are other notable spirits, past and present, who have attempted to educate and inspire our people. We simply have not listened. We have not taken the necessary action to do what is required.

Allow me briefly to expound on my sentiment of the reason why our people have received the harshest of harsh treatments from Europeans.

Our harsh treatment, past and present, seems to be a by-product of European's self-inflicted fears concerning black folks. Their fears exist for no apparent reason other than their ignorance, accompanied by the invisible albatross of guilt hanging around all their necks.

Ignorance and guilt exist within the white race primarily due to the words and actions of their predecessors, ancestors, and founding fathers. It is the documented European legacy of pre-meditated and willful intent concerning slavery. It is their history of Jim Crow Laws and all other indignant behavior, towards black, brown, and melanated people, in America and across the globe.

Their collective ignorance and self–inflicted fears have inevitably produced within their beings an added dimension, that of paranoia. Their historical ignorance, fears, and now their paranoia has resulted in our people sustaining countless unsubstantiated and unwarranted allegations due to the color of our skin. There has been a loss of life, loss of liberty, loss of family, loss of opportunity, loss of finances, and the loss of other comprehensive components of life here in America, as well as those residing in other parts of the world.

Those unconscionable injustices tumultuously played out during America's inception and since. The initial historical words created by their Founding Fathers, framed into their historical legal documents, that speak of processing and displaying high morals, character, and humanitarian features, have produced anything but.

America, and its European conquerors, appear to have acquired, for themselves, a natural, unjustifiable, eternal, profound disdain and hatred of black, brown, and melanated citizens of America for reasons only they can explain.

Their exploitation of our people is common knowledge, and their behavior is perceived today as normal and acceptable for and from them.

Most of us know, believe and subsequently have seen and (or) experienced their creation of their designed, systemic racist system in some form or another.

The irony of it all is that Black folks have NEVER sort out to do any harm nor ill will towards the Europeans who has legitimately earned their rightful recognition (as far as black folks are concerned) as being our natural enemies and oppressors.

Words are powerful, yet in and of themselves are useless if not attached to an action ...

The Quest For Solutions

What are our solutions towards combating a society that's not concerned with leveling the playing field? What are our solutions when America's white citizens are not concerned with the content of one's character?

What are our solutions when co-existing among a people that chooses not to extend the virtue of humanity nor humility towards their fellow human beings, fellow citizens, wherever they may be in the world?

Why have the Europeans chosen the color of one's skin to determine one's place within America's society? In lieu of these human exponents, numerous black and brown folks seem to be motivated toward the challenge of trying to change the hearts and minds of their known enemies and oppressors. They attempt to sway them through their presentations of being rational, and that of a commonsense approach, concerning the race issue in America.

Attempts

Black activists and others bring legalities and facts to the table that are inclusive of evidence.

They bring truth, morals, character, and humanitarian ideologies to their conference table of thanksgiving.

Black folks have embraced their bible and the allegories within as well as their religious doctrines in hopes of seeing and receiving, consistently, their often preached, God like behavior from within the Europeans.

Others bring to the table a spirit of compromise.

Response

Black and brown folks cannot change the hearts and minds of the Europeans. Only they, themselves can do that. Since we have 400+ years to gauge and use as our barometer concerning race relations between the two races, I'm of the opinion that our people 's ongoing, uphill battles/ fight shall continue to manifest itself into the eons of time, giving what we know to be true and factual. "The Dred Scott decision, of 1857"America's Supreme Court ruled, "That blacks had no rights which the white man was bound to respect; and that the negro might justly and lawfully be reduced to slavery ". Today, in this the year of 2023, these words are powerful, yet in and of themselves are useless if not attached to an action. The European's actions, in conjunction with this statement, appears to be that of truth, factual, accompanied by evidence that supports it.

Since the time of our ancestor's evolution from transitioning from being freemen in their native land and those who were living among the aboriginals who were enslaved, we've subsequently contracted the European's virus. Their viral infection among our people has been catastrophic. Their virus has been passed down among our people from generation to generation.

They pursued and captured our ancestors as though they were wild animals. Then they began the indoctrination of infecting their virus into the psyche of our people.Europeans literally brainwashed our ancestors through intimidation, beatings and by torturing them into submission.

Their virus is destroying / killing our people. Due to this historical fact, many of us, especially the younger population, has ultimately incurred their insaneness. The most grievous of example and glaring implication of this insanity that our people have incurred is the unwelcome reality that black folks hurt and kill one another at an alarming rate.

We hurt and kill one another more than law enforcement do. We hurt and kill one another over senseless and trivial matters. Since game recognize game, most of you should recognize the Self-inflicting genocide our people have chosen to participate in.

Yes, it is and always have been a choice. Circumstances aside, we all have choices and free will. All lives do matter which does not exempt nor exclude Black and brown lives. It is totally insane to hurt and kill your own brothers and sisters. Hurting and taking the lives of the very people that are experiencing exactly what you are experiencing, existing in the filth of raciest America.

INSANITY is defined as: the state of being seriously mentally ill. Insaneness reflects having = unsoundness of mind or lack of the ability to Understand.

Conceivably, most gang – bangers   can use as their defense, the insanity plea that releases one from criminal or civil Responsibility.Until we as a people acknowledge and address this fact and begin the construct of healing towards eradicating this viral insanity, nothing else shall matter. I say again, *nothing else shall matter.*

Absolutely, positively, categorically, no victories, large or small against the tyranny black folks face each day from our common enemies shall carry any significance of grandeur nor achievement.   Thus, by not respecting the lives of your own kind, we as a people shall continue to evolve into being, "a lost race of people." That's number one. That is the first and foremost common denominator, characteristic, attitude, and behavior we must exterminate and destroy as a race of people that forever will hinder our upward mobility.

ALL LIVES MATTER, especially of the people that look as you do.

Alfred T. Pyles

Solutions: Reparations / Separations

....Words are powerful, yet in and of themselves are useless if not attached to an action ...

I again ask the question," WHAT are OUR SOLUTIONS?

Answer = Our only viable solutions in my opinion are the acquisitions of both Reparations / Separation.

No matter your status or rank,
no matter your degrees within education,
no matter your financial wealth,
no matter the number of books
           you've written,
no matter the number of philosophical lectures
           you've participated in,
no matter the number of movies
           you've directed or performed in,
no matter your hall of fame status,
no matter the number of business deals
           you've closed on,
no matter,
no matter,
no matter.

If your response to my question is anything other than deliberating for either reparations and (or) separation, know and believe that you are truly living the American dream.

That dream where you're living in an un-bias society, where skin color has no significance of meaning. Where America affords all its citizens, the accessibilities to work, and play on a level playing field.

To those in opposition to my words, I ask:

- Does your commentary includes most black folks throughout this nation?
- Does your commentary galvanize the masses towards a common goal, a common acquisition?
- Or is your commentary simply self-serving, and (or) self-reliant?
- Do your comments, your analysis, your solution (s) reach and (or) affect the common man such as myself?

People such as myself, who holds no status or rank, who possibly are not as highly educated nor sophisticated as you are, we often see no resemblance of an asserted action (s) towards what our people need to do for ourselves, while often times listening to your rendition, concerning the what, when, where, why and how of an issue.

Many of you using hundred-dollar words that most of us can't cash.

But personally, I find it fascinating that in most cases, you all NEVER give the people any tangible resolutions to ponder.

Marcus Garvey offered the people a solution - Back to Africa

Malcolm X gave the people solutions - By Any Means Neccessary

The Black Panther Party exhibited solutions.

Tony Browder, Dr. Claude Anderson, proposed concrete solutions - Eliminate African History Miseducation

Today, we are a reactionary race of people. Never proactive. Constantly talking about what they said, what they alluded to, what they are planning, where they are going, where's the money coming from, where's the money going. On and on and on and on. Same old sh 't. Around and around, the merry go - round /around we go ...where it will stop, nobody knows.

Until most black *folks wake up* and decide that we've had enough of the white man's hypocrisy, and their sinister, and deadly attitudes, and be collectively motivated to bring about change and create nature's paradigm for ourselves, living in America - will continue to be,' Our Hell on earth.

Until all black sororities and fraternities, All black social groups, All black businesses, All black schools, and HBCUs, All black churches, All black entertainers and sports figures, all existing black whatever ...

Until we All, (or most of us) recognize this neutralized, extermination game, recognize that the time has come by way of divine intervention for black people to straighten up our individual backbones and step through the reflective glass pane of cowardness that we've collectively been hiding behind since the time of our Ancestors and forefathers...

 Until we wake – up to the realization that we are in a war of attrition.

A war of conflict. A war that has been designed to gradually eliminate and wear black folks down. It is this racial conflict of a war, of which the European's goal, (by whatever means necessary), is to subject our people into becoming meaningless, insignificant, or minor beings, subjected to their incurable thirst to be rulers over the dark-skinned people of this earth.

Rulers - Towards World Domination

Until we collectively wake – up, it shall be business as usual for the Europeans. The "just be patient tactics "is no longer relevant for our people. That "wait on God "philosophy "has been worn out extensively. It's worn out because the waiting on God philosophy denotes exoneration for black folks towards that of relinquishing any, and all responsibilities of doing …for OURSELVES.
- Do you not know that the Creator has blessed us with a Humanitarian spirit?
- Do you not know that WE are the earthly vessels who are to do the work that we are required to do, that is representatives of our Creator?
- Are you not a representative of your Christian God?

Yes, or know? This ain"t rocket science. It is through US, through our individual as well as collective spirits that our Creator gives us directions that's relative to OUR DOINGS, not our NOT DOING.

"For Whom the Bell Tolls"

Characteristic Differences, Between MAN, and MANKIND

Ernest Hemingway was an American novelist, short – story writer, journalist, and sportsman. *For Whom the Bell Tolls,* was published in 1940. It tells the story of Robert Jordan, a young American volunteer, attached to Republican guerrilla unit during the Spanish civil war.   It possesses the imaginary question of a man who hears a funeral bell, and ask about the person who has died.

The reply to his question is that, because none of us stands alone in the world, each human death affects all of us. Every funeral bell, therefor, Tolls for Thee. This translates into meaning, don't ask for whom the bell tolls "i.e. who died ", because it also tolls for you.When a being dies, theoretically, you also die a little.

I thought it fascinating that this saying, the title, *For Whom the Bell Tolls*, would resonate within my personal spirit. And that, I thought it fascinating it stated within its writing, "i.e., Europeans represents being that of species of mankind".

Man vs Mankind

This segways into my opinionated rendition of the characteristic differences between Man and Mankind. Let's first explore the obvious:

Physical attributes

It's apparent, that there is an obvious physical difference of appearance that exist between the European clan, and those of us who are of African, and (or) Aboriginal lineage.

White: It has become customary to refer to one another as either White, or Black. Neither are white, nor black. Europeans have a different color scheme than us. Their hair is that of flaxen, of the pale, yellow color of dressed flax golden, or red. Europeans' eyes are that of blue, gray, hazel, or green. Their skin is pale, resembling that of an albino.

Black: Among those of us of African and/ or Aboriginal lineage, our color scheme are melanin based, a natural skin pigment. Everyone has some measure of melanin. But it is Our people that have extensively, more melanin than the Europeans. Our hair can be kinky, contrasted with straight, wavy, or curly hair. Afro – textured hair appears denser by nature. In most cases, we have brown eyes, which are dominant. We usually don't have the gene to acquire blue eyes. The reason that you see so much brown is because brown, and black are the dominant colors for all humans, including Europeans.

Clinical research suggests that there exists a distinct difference in odor between the black, brown, melaninated people and the Europeans. Black folks are rhythmic beings and are rhythmically different than our counterpart, the European.

Harmony exists in nature. Our people are harmonic beings.
Our taste in music varies. African music is very rhythmic, with poly rhythms, and is based around more drums, and call – and – response. European music is based more around classical, and instrumentation, with music theory in the bases of what is being played.

Side note: Somewhere I heard that black folk's sphere, (like atmosphere), are of a circular nature. And that the European's are like, more resembled to a square sphere and that our antennas are receptors of energy. Theirs are not like ours.

...Words are powerful, yet, in and of themselves are useless if not attached to an action ...

Europeans are of a different species from that of us who are of African, and (or), Aboriginal lineage.
The word, "Human ", as an adjective, is said to mean:

relating to, or characteristic of people, or human beings . As a noun, Human is distinguished from an animal, (or in science fiction), an Alien.

Close your eyes, and ponder the notion: from the beginning of America's existence ,the history that America have created since its inception. Think upon the white man, and the black man's entangled relationship that has developed, and evolved to this day. Envision the foreseeable future … With eyes closed, through the notion of science fiction, you see the existence of the ever-present Being, walking among us, that logically, WE, (Black folks), can surmise through conjecture, that WE are living among a race people that is from another world.

WE can easily say, through our collective judgement, and final adjudication, that the European clan is of an Extraterrestrial Nature.
That WE, black, brown ,myelinated beings can, and do, readily say to them and, to the universe, without hesitation, that – the European, white man, Caucasian, are of MANKIND / resembling that of a CREATURE.
I am the bearer of distinction. I am the Truth bearer. My truths, My perceptions, My opinions.

For Whom the Bell Tolls

From our ancient past, present, and foreseeable future, it has been said, it has been written, long before my existence, (in my humbled opinion), that the white man is solely, and directly responsible for the ills that existed, and continues to exist, in present day, American society.

Yes, our people have exhibited self – destructive behavior during our time here in America. I know, and believe, that much of our unsavory behavior is primarily due to being a product of our environment. An environment that is racist to its core, prejudice, and discriminatory.

The lack of Quality jobs and opportunities = less jobs, more violence, more jobs, less violence.

The non – existence of a level playing field, and a corrupt system of government, many of us can understand, but not accept the harsh realities of what America is, and always have been.

"Let's make America great again ". So, tell me people, and others like me ... ***When was America great?*** I remember now. America was great when Europeans obtained free land, and incorporated the kidnapping of free men from their native lands, and branded them as slaves, who were to tole the free land that the white man acquired. Got it.

Good vs Evil

Mankind is of evil. I support my opinion based on the story of Adam, and Eve. From that allegory from Christian ideology, one can say, set the stage for the forces of both good and evil to be unveiled. From this unproven hypothetical existence, we shall apply spiritual logic, which suggest that mankind, from that time that's said to exist, was given the opportunity to define in practical application terms, CHOICE. This is when mankind was officially introduced to the concept of engaging, that of having a Choice.

...Words are powerful, yet, in and of themselves are useless if not attached to an action ...

The Action of Eve was offering the forbidden apple to Adam. Adam took the prohibited bite from the apple that Eve presented. The European's Christian bible states: God, having made Adam in his own image, sets them both loose in the garden of Eden with the simple command: you May eat from any tree in the garden, But Do Not eat of the tree of the Knowledge of Good and Evil. The moral of this allegory is, that when people, (Humans), give into their temptation (s), and do that which is commanded Not to do, there are consequences to their Action of Choice.

What was their consequences Sheppard?

Their consequences, (from their Christian bible), is that God said, 'that Adam and Eve would Die. Death was the Almighty 's warning. It appears that, with good, comes evil. Therefore, now with the presence of evil, the loss of innocence takes place. I am of the opinion, that Good, and Evil co – exist. And that Man, and Mankind are given, Universally, by design, from the MOST HIGH, INTENTIONAL leeway in, 'CHOOSING'. Both man and Mankind have been given a command. And the command that's given is simply to Choose. Choose on this day the direction your spirit leads you to.

Speaking to the Christians, as well as All, of whatever your denomination, my spirit has led me to say this to you, a believer of your Christian bible: from the Christian bible, = 1st, Matthew 7: 13 – 14, Enter by the narrow gate. For the gate is wide, and the way is easy that leads to destruction, and those who enter by it are many.

For the gate is narrow and the way is hard that leads to LIFE, and those who find it are few. 2nd, Philippians 4 – 8.

Finally, brothers,
    whatever is true,
    whatever is honorable,
    whatever is just,
    whatever is pure,
is anything worthy of praise, think about these things …

My people, gravitate to that which is SPIRITUAL in Nature … In ALL THINGS.

    "FOR WHOM the BELL TOLLS"
    IT TOLLS FOR THEE …

Hotep / MA 'at

--*Ase'*--

I Too Have Dreams

I too have dreams that one day, in the state of Florida, known for its warm weather, beautiful beaches, and delicious seafood, that the sons and daughters that are either descendants from the continent of Africa or descendants from aboriginal lineage, will be able to sit down together at the table of brotherhood.

I too have a dream that across this nation, our black, brown, and myelinated brothers, and sisters, will call a forever ending truce in regard of the senseless killings and unsavory behavior that Our People have been exhibiting and executing towards the very people that look like themselves. Elders, such as myself, and others within communities across this nation, fear you.

Thug life, from the youngest to the oldest, you should be protecting your family, your neighborhoods, our communities, your people. You should represent being our militia.

That same attitude that most of you have when it comes to your mother, how you will defend her honor at all costs, by any means necessary, is the exact same attitude you should have protecting your own people, your own kind.

The self-inflicting genocide must cease. The violence is out of control, off the chain, and has truly become of epidemic proportions.

All concerned should reflect within themselves and portray outwardly to not only America but portray unto yourselves, as well as the universe that you've self-decreed peace among all those who looks like you, wherever you are. You, me, we're all riding on the same ship, heading somewhere, to whatever destination. We all aspire to arrive alive.

Collectively, we are experiencing the same constant turbulence, one way or another, from the same ocean waves of life. Some of us has risen to the upper most deck. Others find us positioned several decks below. Then, there are those of us who finds ourselves scratching out an existence on the lower most deck, in the hull of the same exact ship, that again, that all of us myelinated beings find ourselves aboard, including the newborn, the small kids, the youths, and young adults.

Young people aspiring to join the thug life, look up to the older thugs, the older so called, want to be gangsters. You, who has chosen to live a life of crime and violence, who seem to think that being incarcerated, relinquishing your freedom to a system of modern-day slavery that have purposefully been created, and designed to take you away from your loved ones, is a fashionable endeavor to brag about. You, who have perpetuated the notion that by going to jail, and (or) prison is somehow an honorable experience to have on your resume. I'm referring to you, in conjunction, who has no problem nor hesitation hurting or taking the life of another of your reflection, deleting them from existence, and destroying lives and families along your way. Your own kinfolk, who are in proximity to you, who were here yesterday, but no longer exist today.

Yes, I too have a dream that our people will awaken and transformed yourselves into being representative of our people, your POWER SOURCE, YOUR JESUS, your CREATOR, or whatever deity you claim.

> YOU, who can be, if you choose to CLAME IT: articulate, a visionary, inspirational, a man, or woman of your word. Then, sends it out unto the UNIVERSE:

> YOU, who can summon within - the creation that you are, from the HIGHEST, - showcasing that you're an HONORABLE PERSON with an Honorable Disposition, that all BEINGS can appreciate and respect. That RESPECT WHICH IS EARNED and not GIVEN.

We cannot appreciate you nor those you've eliminated, for both journeys shall not be complete and fulfilled. The young need and require discipline. The young spirits need and require positive role models. Those young, naive, impressionable, young spirits desperately need, meaningful directions, and positive re-enforcement.

No Man is an island, unto themselves. Each one of us need help, and assistance in becoming productive beings, during one 's existence.

For many of our youths, they find themselves in the commonality of progression. Sadly, disproportionately,

OUR Children travels down, potentially, a beaten path "OF NEVER RETURN. The raw reality is," possibly due to circumstances ", many of OUR CHILDREN begins their applications towards becoming Wards of the state.

The filling out of their application begins by spending time at a juvenile center. Then they progress to their local jail house. Their next adventure shall begin by settling into what they shall call now "their NEW HOME away FROM HOME, where one (whether choosing to, or not), begins their individual, as well as collective, applications for their Doctoral degree - in SURVIVAL.

OUR young brothers and sisters, OUR CHILDREN are crying out to you, and you, and especially you, to come to their aid right now, at this very moment.

Many of these young spirits, minds, and behavior, can be developed into becoming an extraordinary individual, representing their race, their families, and their communities. For me, I know and believe that this dream is the epitome of all other dreams until my duration.

Is there any among you who have had a similar dream as mine?

Is there any among you who concur with the sentiments I've just expressed? If so, say Ase'.

Know and believe, that I'm consciously dreaming at this very moment. I'm dreaming that the words I've just spoken, to those that my words apply to, that most of you, if not all of you, feel what my spirit is trying to communicate.

I'd like to know and believe that most, if not all of you can relate to the foundation of what's required and needed for yourselves and YOUR CHILDREN, your relatives ... OUR CHILDREN. Know and believe that I've attempted to set the tone to what's to become.
From one man to another, RESPECTFULLY. To you also, my Nubian Sisters.

My brothers and sisters, you are their role models. What path shall You choose for yourselves, and for them? They are your sons and daughters, cousins, nieces, and nephews. They are your grandkids, great grandkids, and great, great grand kids. They are our collective future.

Your circumstances are your circumstances. We all have testimonies of experiences of regret. But those experiences does not define the totality of your indispensable qualities. Hurting, killing, and destroying families of those who are the Only allies you have is truly a sign of being mentally ill.

Your choices, as well as your behavior, play directly into the hands of those who have diabolically orchestrated via a system they have specifically created for you.

You already should be fighting against the European virus that will eventually lead us to the brink of insanity. Now you add on the self – inflecting genocide virus. Who among us can withstand that number of viral infections? That amount of mental illness. Who among us can withstand that amount of pressure and think that one is, ok?

Not only are we hurting, and killing one another in the streets, in the jail houses, in the prisons, but people who looks like you are also hurting, and killing our people in controlled environments, such as in hospitals, in shopping centers, and malls, on college campuses, in churches and other public places. Regardless of age, mental illness materializing as mass shootings, is submerged conciously or subconciously in hate. These actions have now become commonplace in our modern-day society, representing present day insantity.

I have dreamed of being the Big Kahuna, (big boss), offering   RESPECTFUL directions, calling out,   both the Crips and Bloods, for the purpose of using them as an example, which many Los Angeles African American street gangs align themselves.

Due to their influence, they could, if they chose, position themselves to be the lead drum majors – that others could follow towards eradicating Black on Black crime.

Their footprints could bring to fruition, the needed alternative, using the blue – prints, left by the Black Panthers. That of self – reliance, self – luv.

A global truce results into Global peace among fellow brethren, wherever they may be in this world.

I too have a dream, that one day, the state of Florida's governor, Ron DeSantis, who mandated a ban on diversity programs in state colleges, will transform himself and his cabinet into the building blocks of freedom and justice, for all its inhabitants, especially for the young, developing minds of academia who are representatives of America's future.

I dream that DeSantis and others will take off their armor of divisiveness and fear, to allow facts and resulting truths concerning the interwoven histories, of both white, and black America, to be that of educational value. And not that of meaningless, due to fear, embarrassment, or shame.

 In this dream, **I dreamed that DeSantis**, during his campaigning for the presidency, that he creates a new version of American history, by lifting the vail of fear, embarrassment, and shame for his people, into that of newly found Honor, particularly for the young, and future generations.

Obviously, that can only happen by presenting a formal apology to the Black, Brown, melanated race of people for the inhumane treatment that historically existed to our Ancestors, forefathers, and even present day violations. Then proceed to promote the long overdue Reparations for Our people, by sitting down at the negotiation table, to hammer out the details. Realizing, that there exists a segment of our people that also desire Separation, from racist America. That is one of my more favorable dreams.

Education is defined as: both the act of teaching knowledge to others and the act of receiving knowledge from someone else. History is a topic of information and knowledge, that is to be taught, received by others, studied, researched, and even debated.

Certain aspects of American, black history, particularly in human affairs, are not to be avoided nor hidden due to your or the governor's own personal feelings. In America, the history of its past mirrors that of the present in many ways. One could say that America's past is synonymous with present day America. That premise should be thoroughly examined, via education.

There are aspects of world history as well as American history that are ugly. Information and knowledge that are not pleasant in and of themselves, but are nevertheless crucial components towards the understanding and learning why the world is the way it is.

Explaining, exploring, why America have been, and is the way it is - today. The histories of both white, and black people, unveils the racially divided.

I've often dreamed that dream, where All people awaken to the obvious realities, and observable trues that have existed through centuries of time. Both histories beg to ask the question: why does race play such an intricate roll in reference to the haves and have nots in America, as well as abroad?

In referencing back to Governor DeSantis, critical thinkers should ask themselves, "Why is the governor so adamant towards not allowing the critical race theory to be taught in the first place?"

I too have a dream that one day in the state of Florida, and in all of America and around the world, that my two adult children, my three grandkids, my nieces and nephews will one day, " truly and factually ", live in a nation where they will not be judged by the color of their skin , but by the content of their character.

I too, have a dream today.
Hat De Oh yes, it is said theoretically, that we all dream. That we have multiple dreams during one's sleeping. You may awaken from your dream and not remember any of that which you've dreamed. But you dream, nevertheless.

I have had that dream, where the young people of present time will not, I say again, will not make the Same Mistakes that their parents, grandparents, great grandparents, great – great grandparents have made, in reference to race relations, here in America.

Young Europeans, young Blacks, "Critical thinking ", in all aspects of life must, be your generation's new and improved mantra, in comparison to the aforementioned. All of you of young minds should know and believe that there exists (to a degree), an element of CORRECT ABILITY from egregious mistakes, generated from past deeds.

No matter the honorable presumptions of validity. Old heads will eventually die. Life and death matters of race, will be in your hands going forward. A need is there, young people as you go forward during your journey through the numerous land mines of life.

Yes, I have dreams ...

I 've dreamed a recurring dream, that the good cops finally muster up the courage to expose and overthrow the bad cops, especially those in disguise as law enforcement officers, who are of the KKK clan. They, who perpetrate unlawful acts, especially upon the black, brown, and myelinated persons residing within the boundaries of this America, supported by their union.

In this disturbing dream, I 'm reminded, that there existed a time when law enforcement were viewed by their previous mission nationwide , as to protect, and serve the citizens of America .Today, law enforcement's sole mission is to represent themselves as being a fraternity, a brotherhood of vigilantes. They are the people 's modern day judges, jurors, and executioners. They often commit heinous crimes against people of color, of which the judicial system routinely, simply exonerated, or are given a mere slap on the wrist.

Within this dream, I've dreamed that all 3 branches of government, as well as all persons, whatever capacity, who has taken a solemn oath to protect and serve the people, inclusive of all others who are representative of the people in whatever capacity, that when the veil of crime, and corruption is lifted and substantiated, that they be swiftly prosecuted and given the harshest of punishment. That ... is definitely, if I must say so myself - a dream.

I also have had a **dream turn into a nightmare.** Like the nightmare that shows my people continually denouncing their heritage, their lineage, their spirituality. My nightmare suggest that a great number of my people are simply afraid to transcend or transform from / to that which is meant and designed for them.As the old saying goes, "what's for them – is for them ...What's for you -is for you.

Somewhere I heard that no religion could teach you what the universe has already instilled in you. Man = made religion. Religion did not make man ...The Truth is in man, not in religion. Our Creator is in us, not in their religion, their Christianity. I've lived a dream.

In this dream that I've lived, the dream revealed that I'm a living spirit that does not choose to hope. I also do not choose to have faith. For, I am a living spirit who choose to Know and Believe. In this dream, I know and believe that the taking down of historical monuments that we perceive to be disrespectful as well as racist does not change our plight.

In this dream, I know and believe that parades, festivals, and luncheons are simply symbolisms of historical accomplishments, but they don't change our present realities.

That, I know, and believe that religion / Christianity was beaten into the psych of our people minds. That, I know, and believe, that my people fear, positive, revolutionary changes. That, I know, and believe, that for every two steps forward that our people take, the European's system collaborate among themselves, strategist measures, that knock our people back 10 / 20 years in most cases.

Another dream of mine reveals to me, that a Modern Day Miracle is needed, which can only be summoned through our collective spirits ...towards our collective actions, is needed. The phenomenon of a miracle in most cases are unexplainable. The phenomena of nature are exactly that, unexplainable.

Every day we all experience those miracles of nature. We feel, hear, smell, taste and touch nature in some form or another. The miracles of nature are exclusive of input from all beings.

A Modern Day Miracle is Needed for Our People, living in this 21st century. It's needed for all, of America.

Yes indeed, let me mention the dream that sees the young, of black, and white grow up. One race Representing the Oppressed, while the other race represents being the Oppressor.

Due to both races, abilities to obtained information and knowledge, particularly matters concerning HUMANITY, and HUMILITY, both, "through the powers vested in them", chooses resolutions, over conflict.

This dream indicated to me that these young spirits will understand the need to break the chain of DIVISIVENESS. If breaking the chain is humanly unrealistic, due to the systemic nature of things, just maybe, they will at least recognize, and RESPECT TRUTHS and facts enough to make whole a people who has been historically downtrodden. For me, it shall represent the concept, that of incurring a Silver lining, of historical proportions, that I'll take any day of the week.

Always, there shall be Inquiring minds, who knows, that an existing, outstanding debt, with interest, is OWED, that we, today are bound to collect. Yet, possibly, it appears that the debt may never be paid during the life time of the baby boomer generation.

Finally, from the accumulation of the totality of my dreams, we as a people *will get to the promise land.*

But my dream suggests, that to get to that promised land, it shall only occur through our own efforts with Our Creator being our navigator.

Dreams, often times, unexpectedly, do come true.

We have the abilities. We have the responsibilities - to DO for OURSELVES. No force outside of ourselves is going to do a damn thing for us. It is through spiritual forces, that lies within everyone of OUR PEOPLE, that shall compel our victories as well as our defeats. The only way to win, to be victorious is to compete. We are and have always been the underdog. If we choose not to compete, then we choose not to defend. Which means that we possess no defense. Which means, that we as a body of people, will again, be totally vulnerable to the whims of our known enemy and oppressors.

Compete or die trying ... Our Creator is and always shall be our eternal, internal supreme navigator.

Compete or die trying ...

--*Ase'*--

This portion of my commentary is dedicated to Mr. Clinton Oliver. For me, inspiration occurred due to his insight, foresight, and through his spirit.

Monologue

America, the land of immorality, have chosen to be a divisive proponent against TRUTH and FACTS vs the fabrication of them both. History has spoken. History is speaking. And unbeknownst to each one of us, History shall continue to speak. What shall the variables be pertaining to that coming history?

Note: To ALL Mankind BEINGS, who legally are defined as through your own definition and interpretation as being European, as well as those desiring to be viewed and considered European, you are ALL IMMAGRANTS, from a land that is not of this land. Your original Origin is not of here, on this stolen land that Europeans have named America.

A day of RECKONING SHALL BE UPON YOU. Shall BE UPON US ALL. Regardless of religious choice or beliefs, a reckoning awaits.

To my black, brown, and myelinated brothers and Sisters, especially those of us of the baby boomer generation of which I am affiliated, it is my humble opinion that WE have failed in developing the necessities towards cultivating our distinct culture that we were obligated to cultivate.

We've not developed our minds nor our capacities through our own efforts to stand apart from our known enemy and oppressor, but instead has collectively chosen to emulate and imitate them in all conceivable manners.

It appears also that we have chosen to live off the backs of our Ancestors as well. Those who endured the harsh realities of life during slavery and Jim Crow while existing in raciest America.
They who were burdened with sacrifices that we've never had to face nor endure.

They who fought when they had to and died when they didn't, for simply seeking the respect that alluded them.
They, who were assaulted for desiring the manifestation of the high moral words that had been written on paper.

Today, most of us has sacrificed nothing, fought for nothing nor have many of our people died for any honorable purpose, specifically that of the uplifting of our own people.

We've generally become complacent and satisfied with the life we're living and feel no obligation, need or desire to rock the boat of contentment. Casualties nevertheless continue to exist daily for all the wrong reasons.

Here and now, I Acknowledge and give a shot out of Respect, Honor and Admiration to those Freedom Fighters, Revolutionaries who has given their lives, usually involuntarily, and to the existing human spirits who has given a large portion of their adult lives, fighting to improved and create a better America within the set parameters and guidelines of a systemic racist government and society. I applaud you individually as well as collectively. Representing those that agree with me, We Thank You, We SALUTE YOU ALL.

To all of Man and Mankind, LOOK WHERE WE ALL ARE. Co-existing in a pool of filth concerning our human conditions, based on skin color. Two words come to mind that describe our ongoing saga living in America. Those two words are DIVISIVENESS, and Inhumanity.

Personally, I'm sick and tired of being sick and tired of politicians, academia, historians, philosophers, intellectuals, clergy, entertainers, civil right leaders, talk shows, athletes, and all others who chime in daily, speaking on the racial disparities of America's society.

Humans, that of mankind, who are thought to be of a higher species of animal purposefully, intentionally have chosen the continuation of a diabolical trajectory of being inhuman, and divisive towards black and brown people.

Note: Europeans, white people, Caucasians, Have the Right to choose to be raciest. I, representing black folks (who agree with my views), also *have the right to choose not to be associated* / affiliated with those who have chosen to be racist, and exhibit raciest views. Now, what part of that statement do you take issues with?

Through our divine and eternal nature, black folks have shown the Europeans, the world, and its universe, a degree of greatness that lies within our people. To still be standing, and to still be relevant in the grand scheme of things, we as a people have exemplified perseverance and resiliency, that is not yoked with any other form of human, that has ever walked the earth.

We, as a race of people should build upon that legacy. I'm of the belief that building upon that legacy shall require us to Listen. We should revisit and listen to what our ancestial predecessor's pedigree have said. It is mandated for us to be still and listen. If you haven't listened to your inner spirit in the past, then do so now. The time is upon us.

Our Ancestors are seeking our attention. Purposefully, and intentionally, listen to seek divine instructions through your individual as well as our collective Spirits, concerning your life, and the lives of others. Listening to your spirit (I've grown to know and believe) cradles you into the council of your ancestors / our ancestors. Cradles you and I into the resting place of HUMANITY, within our Souls. Consciously or subconsciously, Divineness, WE REPRESENT. Divineness YOU ARE.

The next glaring subject matter I'd like to expound upon concerning our ineptitude towards not formulating our own culture is directly related to the individual choices we've chosen in desiring to be accepted or embraced by Europeans.

You see, we've been forced fed their interpretation of civilization, their society, their system of government, their way of life, their immoralities, their customs, their traditions, their heritage, their ideologies, their mannerisms, their language, their impersonation of integrity, their characteristics, their habits, their appearance and dress, their celebratory events and even more importantly their religions.

We've more often than not embraced their ways for the sole purpose of conforming, desiring to being accepted in the fabric of mainstream, white society. But for the most part, our efforts have been futile.No matter how much nor how often you try, no matter the honorable accomplishments you've obtained, the mountains you've climbed or the obstacles you've overcome, the manners you've extended, the patterns you've created, or the level of competency you've displayed.

Included are those numerous occasions - where you find yourself in proximity of your known oppressors, where you activate within your mind, the acting out of performance, delivering your presentation, your version of race relationship. I'm speaking of when you're interacting among white people: From the very beginning of this ordeal, your mind and body speak to you. Both elements simultaneously begin to tolerate the experiencing of the - illusions of inclusion.

We all feel it in some way or another. It's a natural feeling. It's that feeling that can swell within for the very reason, that at some point in time in your conscious mind, you remember past events, or have experienced, firsthand, recent circumstances, that reminds you of America's apartheid, (a crime against humanity). Thus, lies an innate, internal distrust towards your European mates, while swirling into the dichotomy, (contrast between two things, like war and peace / love and hate) of the illusion, of inclusion.

That feeling which derives from the fact that you know within, that you and your race of people have had to fight for the opportunity to be standing where you're standing at that very moment. Engaging the European, male, and (or) female, where once upon a time, we feared reprisal for a handshake, or an embrace.

Somewhere within your being, you remember that people have lost their lives fighting for justice, fighting for human rights.
Those human rights that have been literally and figuratively given at birth to others. Through it all, it appears, (generally speaking) that our efforts and fight towards gaining equality seems to have never produce the Respect that's warranted from the beginning of human life.

One cannot change the hearts of man. Humans must change. You cannot legislate morality, today, tomorrow, nor in the future.

Morality is defined as: the belief that some behavior is right and acceptable, and that other behavior is wrong. Morals and ethics must be taught, and exhibited to all beings, all human life.

....Words are powerful, yet, in and of themselves are useless if not attached to an action....

Doing unto others as you would have them do unto you, appears to carry no moral significance of meaning within the white race.

Personally, I am irritated and exhausted from listening and reading through all mediums about the comfortability of which the white man attempts to tell our story and our struggles towards not being accepted as a viable member of their mainstream America. They absolutely, have no problem interviewing, reporting that of data, or even giving their commentary concerning racial issues, between blacks, and whites.

Yet they, and black folks that have a public platform, appear to never offer people any substance of suggestions in regard of viable solutions or alternatives to the racial injustices black people incur every day of our lives existing in their raciest white America.

Talking about what Americans need to do often evoke the simple words, "Can we all just get along?" that have no committed actions attached. Its evident when Europeans get down – right belligerent when their history is called into question. Attached to their belligerence, is their present-day attempts to suppress, deny, and ignore their history.

Europeans have always run from their truth. But, of course, "THEY CAN NOT HIDE".

As in nature, there exist times where the bear and the wolf eat side by side. The one thing that they do not naturally do is to cohabitate. Ray Charles and Stevie Wonder, both can see that this society has never and shall never truly worked for us. Absolutely, there is no legislation, no speech, no religion, no sermon, no ritual, no prayer, that can undo nor do what is required and needed from man, and mankind to harmoniously coexist. As we continully live out our lives living an illusion of inclusion.

Objectives are CLEAR. Always has been. If we haven't figured it out in 400 plus years, what makes you legitimately think or even believe that an equal playing field will ever become the norm? We know very well who the black man's common enemies and oppressors are. We as black folks, simply do not know who we are.

WHAT IS OUR SOLUTION?

Are we, (Man / Mankind), not interested in finding a viable solution to the race problem?

Does there exist an unwritten notion, among the black elite, as well as the present-day bourgeois' (middle class) blacks, concerning individually, getting pleasure from their abilities to intellectually engage, to figuratively spar - verbally with the European?

Now - a – days, it appears, it's simply the fashionable thing to do. Even when you win the verbal jousting, what tangible, substantially significance do your presentation produce, for our people?

Do black folks, as a race of people, do we truly and legitimately have the necessary and needed power to bring about change? This for me is the inevitable LIFE and DEATH question for all of Man and Mankind living/ residing on the planet earth. What are our collective, intended solutions, concerning race, here in America?

If, collectively desire a solution to the race problem that exist here in America, my opinion suggests that the black man's search for an answer seems to have continuously reverted back to the days of slavery to present day. His search has been totally saturated in investing into the dependency upon praying, hoping, and having faith the size of a mustard seed that God will do.

That God will prevail.

That God will straighten that which is crooked.

That God will do for the melanated people residing in America as well as those residing in other sectors of the world.

Is praying, hoping, and having faith that God will affect the white citizens, and all entities thereof, and direct mankind to repent, embrace truth and facts concerning America's histories, past, present, and future productive?

That god will alter the minds within the American government on all levels and all its representatives. That through God's intervention, the white race will finally be storing the overdue sentiment of a formal apology and make amends for the wrongs that has been done referencing the divisive, and inhumane   treatment of black and brown, melanated men, women, as well as, often times, unjust treatment of our children, residing on native's land since America's inception.

We have been impatiently waiting for the Europeans and all those who have chosen to be viewed as a European – that they will transcend into experiencing a PARADIGM SHIFT among themselves. Waiting for them to exhibit a fundamental change in their approach and underlying assumptions towards black and brown people.

Europeans have created this quagmire (a dangerous place), and have harvested within their collective minds, justifications of their insanity regarding the brutal and unjust treatment of our people.

We somehow want to believe that the European's hearts will miraculously, collectively exhibit through manner, deeds, and expression, the due respect that's warranted to the black and brown citizens.

It has been a common occurrence since the days of our ancestors and forefathers and those of us present-day even, that we're continually subjected to abuse from those who believe that it is their right to rule over the dark people of the earth.

Inhumanity, and divisiveness are their tools of choice towards maintaining their stronghold. The European defines the word, "Humanitarian" as: concerned with or seeking to promote human welfare. For the British Red Cross, a humanitarian is a person who prevents and alleviates human suffering wherever it may be found."

Europeans, I personally would like to believe that exhibiting humanitarian features lies somewhere within most of you. But in my humble opinion, subsequently it appears that you possess an innate nature of evil.

How else can you explain the history you've created? The history you are presently creating. I've wondered what standard of measurement do you use that justifies your kind to be that of an honorable race of people?

Your God, that's of the variety of father, son and holy spirit is said to be the orchestrator of your individual / collective lives. If so, your belief system, your power source has sanctioned all the atrocities of inhumanities towards the dark people of the earth, (documented and undocumented) for the past 400 + years.

That shocking, appalling time in history, as well as present-day, has afforded your white race great power. And that power has continuously generated, through your blood lines enormous resources, and wealth. In conjunction, you've garnered yourselves white privileges that most of you have mapped out, planed out, and have always taken advantage of.

Today, the schizophrenic Caucasian's race, and all those desiring to be viewed and approached as being of the Caucasian persuasion, know that the residue of power, and wealth, acquired from your ancestors and founding fathers, is directly due to their obtaining FREE land and forcible FREE LABOR to tole their land, for centuries.

You all today, have benefited tremendously from the events of that time in your recorded history. Yes, you yourselves of present-day have absolutely nothing, what-so-ever to do with what happened back then. That does not eliminate the fact that you benefit from it - all the days of your lives.

But....if there was ever a time in history, where all ethnic groups, for the most part (compared to any other increment of time in American history) have co – mingled, and have lived, grown up together, and attended school together, its now.

If there was ever a time in history, where the baby boomers and all those thereafter, should potentially be wiser than those who came before us, its now.

All people should have grown to a higher plain of consciousness, concerning the need of expressing Unity, and HUMANITY towards all people of this universe. Most people living in this America today should be more sensitive towards the systemic racism culture that exist. You would think America would have matured by this time in its history.

Referencing back to the enormous resources and wealth you've accumulated; it openly appears that the white race has generated among yourselves unconscionable greed, that prohibits present day Europeans from seeking redemption from past as well as present wrong doings.

This is all about you, present-day Europeans more so than anything else. This is about this present time in history, that you're forming your legacy, that all of you are creating, that's not that of your ancestors nor founding fathers.

Without further ado, I concur with those with like minds and present to others my personal, SPIRITED overview of what I personally believe to be our only viable solutions to the skin color racism dilemma, that saturates our human experience here in America and abroad.

SOLUTION: Reparations / SEPARATION
A grassroot perspective...

I shall not attempt to quantify reparations. There are those among us who are thoroughly and accurately more qualified to do so. But, I shall say that I know and believe that the black, brown / melanated beings residing here in America, whether a descendant from Africa or that of aboriginal lineage, that we are certified, qualified, and shall exemplify to America, and to the universe, our ancestors/ forefather's legacies. They are forever to be honored, and held up to the highest esteem, and given the unadulterated respect, that are due and owed, historically to them and to our people.

Just as Europeans today benefit from their historic past, we too shall benefit from our people's collective sufferings, and miseries, brought forth by the actions of those of European's lineages.

Morally and legally, we have evidence, precedence, and proof that substantiate our certifiable-ness, qualifiable-ness, and exemplification of eligibility.

Words are powerful, yet in and of themselves are useless if not attached to an action...

How often have you heard that we will never receive reparations? Religious and spiritual people often say that one should speak [whatever] into existence.

That life and death are in the power of the tongue. So, to those that say that we'll never receive reparations, you are correct. We shall never receive reparations for the simple fact that we speak death towards the acquisition of it. It's that simple. If we don't collectively speak life towards acquiring reparations, or anything else which is honorable, and in this case morally and legally due and owed to our people, via OUR ANCESTORS, and forefathers sufferings, our honorable endeavor shall never manifest into a reality.

What part of that statement that you don't understand?

And to those who are against receiving reparations, why do you choose to manufacture and then justify your personal need to oppose / derail others pursuit in obtaining and receiving reparations? One is either for or against.

You shall appear to represent that old stereotype of being those crabs in a barrel. Those crabs attempting, trying as best they can to escape certain death while other crabs go all out to pull the attempting escapees back down to await their fate. [As we continure to use this analogy to define ourselves, we should not condem the desire to live, but those who put us in the barrel.]

You're either on the side of righteousness or you're an advocate for the racist system that opposes making amends for a wrong Europeans has done - putting us in the barrel. Not only are reparations owed, but reparations are also required and more important are a necessity for the black and brown people that has been historically downtrodden through the hands of the white race and their distasteful, repugnant, scandalous, systemic, raciest system.

As an individual, one has the right to reject receiving reparations. Simply reject or give the proceeds back. You nor your family possibly don't approve, need nor desire to be a recipient. But you do not have the right to block others that look as you do, through whatever means of receiving, just because you're not in agreement towards the historical implications it shall create. Shut up and go about your business. Be Neutral, if anything. Merely a suggestion. Is that so hard to do?

For once in your adult life, you do not have to volunteer as their house nigger, standing on the side of your white master, blocking, disrespectfully, that which is owed, and due. Due from acts of slavery, Jim crow, including present-day injustices, placed upon our people.

If you choose publicly to voice your displeasure, concerning your disagreement toward your people receiving reparations, I truly desire that you go on public record, and make yourselves known to all. We need not mistake you for another. We need to know exactly who you are, and which side of the fence you're on. We need to know now and for all time. A day may come, that you need your people to support you, in some way or another. Don't be another O.J.

Note: In my opinion, the absolute reason that our people can not focus on life's more serious pertinent issues concerning reparations and our upward mobility, is that we are earnestly DISTRACTED by ALL the social media, (Instagram, Twitter (X), Facebook, Pinterest, and LinkedIn), movies and TV shows that black folks simply plays token roles, sports, social clubs, and social activities, and any, and ALL other discretionary elements known to man, and mankind.

Distractions continues to grow. Until we as a people recognize this as being factual and make a conscious decision not to be distracted, by shutting all the BS that is around you down, we shall never be able to achieve, collectively, the upward mobility that we so desperately need for our people. We need to actively, and with purpose, jump on the bandwagon for justice, of which we need, Right Now.
  JUSTICE ...
  What do We Need = Justice
  When do we need it = Right Now.

Note: I do not understand how individual states can get away with suggesting, or offering monetary reparations to the black citizens of that state, and think that will/should be the end of righting a wrong, making amends to all America's black, and brown citizens, who are morally, and legally authorized to receive.

Even more so, I do not understand how black citizens would consider accepting such an offer. How does that process benefit all other black, brown, melanated beings, who are descendants of Africa, and/or aboriginal lineage residing in other American states.Reparations should be distributed through the Federal Government, the catholic church, and the many European wealthy banking families, Period.

From a common man's perspective, what methods would I choose to initially get us at the negotiation table with our known enemy and oppressor?

Solution: *Boycott*

I'll begin with two boycotts. One old, one new. The old suggest boycotting mass transportation. We should withdraw from all public forms of transportation as they did back in the Montgomery boycott (Dec.5, 1955- Dec. 20,1956).

The new method that I suggest is specifically targeting and geared towards the entertainment industry. Any form of entertainment that we provide to the public should cease.

Sports, specifically basketball and football, are by far are addictions that I believe white America have grown accustomed to and enjoy.

As for football, since the days of legendary football coach Paul "Bear "Bryant of Alabama and his teams that were segregated (all white), were extremely reluctant to integrate. September 12, 1970, USC played a game against the all-white Alabama Crimson Tide in the state of Alabama. Alabama lost 42-21. Coach Bryant stated afterwards (paraphrasing), "I have to get me some of them", referring to black ball players on USC's football team. Ever since that time in history, southern most states football programs would be forever changed.

On average, both collegiate, professional basketball and football teams, consist predominantly of black players. The revenue generated from these sports teams have grown expeditiously and are off the chain.

Know and believe that Europeans will adamantly defend both game's revenues. Make no mistake about it. Money is the European's God. Mess with the white man's abilities to generate revenue for himself and his clan, there's going to be repercussions and consequences. No ifs, ands and buts about it.

I propose from pop Warner, junior high, high school, college, to the professional ranks, shut it down at least for the amount of time it will take for the powers to be inspired or compelled to agree to come to the negotiation table in good faith to negotiate the initial terms of engagement.

Then follow-up by getting to the meat and bones of the specified life and death issues concerning our people. In this case, paying their overdue bill with interest to our people. Whatever amount of time may be needed to initially to boycott, to whatever the next legally and peaceful form of demonstration our people choose to speak to a life and death, never give up attitude. This is vitally crucial to retain and to sustain for the success of our people, not only for ourselves, but more importantly for the generations to come.

I chose all the entertainment industry, especially sports, specifically that of basketball, and football because that is where the most money is generated in my opinion. Most of us regular folks would consider giving up a limb for the type of money these entertainers and athletes receive today.

In my opinion, if there exist any group of workers who should be able to withstand unemployment for an indefinite period, that's receiving a weekly, bi-weekly, or monthly check for their survival, it's the entertainment / sports industry.

For those of you who has been existing and sitting or standing on the sidelines all your lives while others have been on the front lines fighting to create the opportunities you enjoy, this time in history has come to YOU, YOU, and YOU, and to ALL of man.

This is my opinion, my suggestion.
If you have a better one, let's hear it.

Note: Europeans, the time has come for your race to pay the piper. My black and brown relatives, the time has come for us to demand that the piper be paid in full. It shall be an honorable endeavor to all concerned. It's doable. It's an endeavor that shall benefit all of man and mankind, for generations to come.

Our actions, not our words shall in fact change the course of American history and universal history. That change, that alternant resolution that's required to preserve the sanctity of life, liberty, and the pursuit of happiness.

The time has been long overdue to Awaken and become consciously aware and listen to our inner spirit(s), which should inspire us all to seek resolutions/solutions towards the unscrupulous race problems of which the only human antidotes that's available for the healing process to begin, on both sides are readily available.

The antidotes prescribed for the Europeans are acceptance of TRUTHS, FACTS, and knowing that you are legally and morally obligated to make whole a displaced, race of people that desperately requires the attention for this to be so.

Then focus on your own salvation/redemption.

The only prescription of antidote that's prescribed for the displaced black and brown people residing in America and abroad is to know and believe that their European virus is real, and it will presumably continue to infect us presently and in the future. We will display some form of their virus in divert ways.

We must address our collective denial concerning our illusions of inclusion and that their God, their Jesus, their Holy spirit will do for the black and brown people all the duties that black and brown people should be doing for ourselves.

You see, many of us continue to choose to live a fairytale of existence. We've chosen the idea to be patient and continue to pray, hope and have at least the amount of faith the size of a mustard seed. That strategy has been the adopted formula that we think will eventually change and alter the hearts of mankind, the Europeans.

We must do for ourselves. We must do for ourselves through the guidance and directions of our individual and collective spirits. I'm told that's called connecting through our SPIRITUALITY. Spirituality is that divine communication that has literally sustained our people all these years whether we consciously know this or not.

But more is needed than sustainability, than endurance, than to tolerate. Our collective spirituality requires regenerative practices (able to or tending to regrow, or be renewed, or restore, especially after being damaged, or lost). Our people have both been for centuries.

We are the earthly representatives walking the earth. It is through our collective beings that the manifestation of our creator flows through and is dispense throughout the universe. It directs our actions which displays one's character of heart and not that of the color of one's skin. We are the earthly vessels representative of OUR CREATOR that is of SPIRIT.

We too need the antidote of the acceptance of truth and facts in conjunction of the obligation we all have in the remembrance of our *ancient ancestors and, forefathers,* whom all have paid the ultimate price concerning their quality of life or the lack thereof. These antidotes are, in my opinion, the only pure, natural remedies to the European virus that can cure our people psychologically, intellectually, and spiritually.

The actions that we are required to eradicate their virus from within our people, shall eventually enable our collective ability to take off the cloak of our denial concerning a culture that is not of ours, and allow us to think outside the box of the mental bondage that we've acquired through indoctrinations.

There exists no other available prescription suitable nor effective enough that has the power to ultimately alter the mankind created collision course of Morality vs Divisiveness. Undoubtedly there are sacrifices to be made from all who know and believe this to be an honorable truth and endeavor. I firmly believe that once this game plan begins to take root, it will galvanize all people that has a vested interest towards avoiding becoming extinct.

Many people believe it is an impossibility for America's created and manufactured civilization to cease to exist. History begs to differ.

Reparations can take numerous forms, including affirmative actions, individual monetary payments, settlements, scholarships, waiving of fees or debt, systemic initiatives to offset injustices, land-based compensation related to independence, apologies, and acknowledgements of the injustices and more. [perpetural stream of income like cacinos]

ALL ROADS LEAD BACK TO TRUTH

...Words are powerful, yet in and of themselves are useless if not attached to an action...

Science: Google states that science has always been defined by its disciplines, by its areas of focus, study, training, specialties, and subject matters. Science is a branch of knowledge or study dealing with a body of facts or truths systematically arranged and showing the operation of general laws. It is said that science generates solutions for everyday life and helps us to answer the great mysteries of the universe.

A truth concerning science is that science cannot help solve the mystery of the universe, concerning Racism. You see racism is not a mystery. "Google, via David R. Roediger (What is a social construction?) states that RACE is a human-invented, shorthand term used to describe and categorize people into various social groups based on characteristics like skin color, physical features, and genetic heredity. Race is a real social construction that gives or denies benefits and privileges.

America spends an abundant amount of time, energy, and money talking about race and its byproducts, as of prejudice, discrimination, or antagonism directed against America's citizens (historically speaking) who are not of European descent. Yet, Europeans have the audacity to question black folks patriotism in this country after all they have put our people through, past, present, and future.

The past determines our future in so many ways and history has and is continuing to teach all of us that the white man has never attempted to correct past misdeeds and harm.

What possible reason or motive should black, brown, and red men of the earth believe that white men will do anything willingly to make amends for the obvious wrongs they've perpetrated? I've noticed that Europeans often are the ones telling our stories of which they are representees of the very people that we call our enemies and oppressors.

We, who are melanated, are the recipients of your European-created Racism. You create Movies, documentaries, symposiums, and numerous other presentations, allowing speeches by all races discussing the ills of our society. All medium of communication at their appointed time speak on the subject, with guests of all nationalities. And these people come on and speak so eloquently about the horrors of racism and the crimpling effects it's still producing over centuries TO OUR SOCIETY.

But they never speak of a solution. Because the solution to America's race problem can't be eradicated by manmade laws. Nor from Praying, nor from a church sermon, nor marching, nor from any form of protest. None of those types of actions will eliminate Racism.

The solution to the eradication of racism can only occur when White America chooses to confront its history face to face. Admit the wrong that was done. They must at least attempt to make amends, and then proceed to repent by cleaning their hearts, souls, minds, and spirits up to reflect a more genuine degree of HUMANITY within themselves, and to all people.

First, this isn't rocket science. And because it's not, is the very reason it shall NEVER HAPPEN. It shall never happen simply because people in general, Europeans specifically CAN'T HANDLE THE TRUTH.

ALL ROADS LEAD BACK TO TRUTH.

America is unable, unequiped to deal with the truth concerning their history. So, STOP LOOKING FOR Racism TO MIRACULOUSLY DISAPPEAR. It never will. The character of the European race won't allow it. Their thirst for power and their inability to face and handle the Truth just won't allow it.

There are some good, decent white folks living in America and abroad. But it's not enough of them to make a difference. Truth: The truth is that collectively, the European race of people has evil characteristic traits that seemingly have developed and evolved into being their NATURE. Evil is now their DNA.

On this Sunday evening, I watched a segment on 60 minutes, of which they were discussing the horrors that the native Americans were presented in Canada back in the day at this boarding school. The catholic church, the priests, and nuns performed the most hideous acts upon the children of various tribal ancestry.

A slogan was created for the children which said," KILL THE INDIAN IN THE CHILD." The report also revealed many deaths of aboriginal children caused by the very people who were there to oversee the development of the native children. I'm talking about children. Of course, that development directive consisted of the European brainwashing native children as with the native adults.

As with our ancient African ancestors, the native aboriginal men, women, and children, the European way of life was forced fed. The European customs, language, and traditions. During the forced transformation at this school for the Indian children, rape, sodomizing, and murder were commonplace throughout their stay. Again, the most hideous of acts upon children coming from and being administered by God's so-called people, the Catholics, and Christians.

These so-called priests and nuns have been molesting children for centuries. Pastors, ministers, deacons, and church administrators all over this nation and around the world are more dirty than clean, all in the name of their God. Don't get angry at me. If the shoe fits, damn-it- wear it. If not, these words don't apply to you.

In America and other places in this world, the color of one's skin determines their place in life. Ouachita Baptist Univerisity, June 23,2020 - J. Danny Hays: *Created in the image of God*: I quote, "Any serious biblical study of race or ethnicity should start in Genesis 1. Their bible does not start off with the creation of a special or privileged race of people. When the first human being is created, he is simply called Adam, which is Hebrew for" humankind." God is said not to be in human form, but rather, that humans are in the image of God in their moral, spiritual, and intellectual nature.

Note: I'm referring to the European bible, for this book is what we've been forced fed for centuries. This is also the book that's over all other books as the divine word of God. A reminder that the Bible is a book of allegories, and is not to be taken or received literally, but more so, figuratively. It's also a book of contradictions. The Bible does possess some moral, spiritual, and intellectual teachings and life lessons through its stories and parables. The teachings and lessons are presented in words, which can be Powerful, but in and of themselves are useless and (or) destructive if not attached to good actions. Actions of godliness, actions of humanity, to all of man and mankind.

The Europeans have indeed attached action to their words, but their actions are not of good nor godliness. So, why would you choose, knowing their history, knowing your history, hook your wagon up to a people that represents Evil?

Why would you believe anything that comes out of their mouths?
Pale Face Does Speak with Fork Tongue. A Fact that has been proven time and time, and time again.

All roads lead back to Truth.

The Truth is that the Europeans have chosen to harvest, not that of their own deity's moral, spiritual, and intellectual nature, but that of their creation, choosing to harvest a nature representative as being Hypocritical, Despicable, Vile Diabolical.

Europeans can not be trusted. For example, they have propagandized the world as to Adam (as in Adam and Eve), being the first human, mankind, when scientific facts suggest that the oldest known evidence for modern humans are fossils found at Jebel Irhoud, Morocco, dated about 360,000 years old. Adam supposedly lived between 120,000 and 150.000 years ago. That's over a 200-thousand-year difference. So, how can Adam be the first human born in the Garden of Eden?

In the movie, *A Few Good Men*, the actor Jack Nicholson said, "YOU CAN'T HANDLE THE TRUTH." That was an assumption. Google defined the word assumption as, a thing that is accepted as true or as certain to happen. It is certain to happen, because it's been happening from the imprisonment of our African ancestors until this very moment, that America Can't Handle the Truth.

> *You can't speak for everyone, so speak for yourself.*
> *Can you handle the Truth?*

What is certain to happen is that Europeans will simply fabricate and ignore the historical truth and facts. Truth is too painful for Europeans. Let me put the truth question to test. What is *your truth* knowing the historical documented legal history concerning America's beginning? This question concerns Christopher Columbus setting foot on native land. You must have an opinion one way or another. What is *your truth* about the facts of Columbus's so-called discovery?

Next, what is *your truth* concerning slavery and ALL the documented evidence of its existence? Speak up…Again, you must have an opinion, one way or another…

What is *your truth* concerning the dismantling of the African family?

What are your thoughts concerning Africans being stripped of their freedom, their language, their culture, and their deity?

What are your thoughts about being striped of anything and everything that you cherish, at this very moment?

Allow me to get back to the *family*…. Oh, the *family* that you Europeans so fondly interject into the mainstream fabric of society that's incorporated into everything that's seemingly wholesome and good.

You speak love for *family*. Every sports team is representative of a *family*. Every business of multiple people is representative of a *family*. Every church, religious group, temple, mosques, and synagogue represent *FAMILY*. Every gang, every social group, every sorority, and fraternity is representative of *family*. All groups of people of a bloodline or no bloodline at all, refer to themselves as a *family*.

Yet, Europeans destroyed black, brown, and red *FAMILIES*, and showed absolutely no remorse for doing so. Today, Europeans feel no responsibility, accountability, or obligation to the Black, Brown, and Red people of today for that time in history, in the destroying our people's families, which for the white mankind being is Mainstream America's most sacred element known to man and mankind: *THE FAMILY.* During slavery, African *family* members were set apart, detached, disconnected from one another, and splattered into the four corners of the earth.

Soon out of the mother's womb, a newborn baby was taken away from its mother before she ever held her child. And if she was fortunate enough to have held her child, often, the newborn child would be snatched from her arms and transported somewhere far away from its birth mother, birth father, and siblings. Those hideous acts have been told historically numerous times. European women, European families, role-play that scenario and imagine the pain that mother, father, and siblings must have felt. They could do absolutely nothing to prevent it from happening.

Today in the year 2023, I, as a black man, and our race of people, should harbor no ill will toward your ancient ancestors, founding fathers, or forefathers for the evil they've perpetrated upon our people. Nor should we as a people display ill will towards Europeans of today, for our people living in a systemically racist, society. Much disparity still exists which continues to showcase inhumane treatment towards our people that affects us today, and will continue to affect us in adverse ways, seemingly forever. Unless you collectively finally see the need for America to heal.

Put yourselves in our shoes. The word is EMPATHY, "The ability to understand and share the feelings of another."

What Europeans exhibit, more than not is, APATHY, "a lack of interest, enthusiasm, or concern."

Having the acquired historical knowledge that our people were tortured, and brutalized in the most barbaric manner ever known to the species of man and mankind, yet there's been no overt, official apology from America's government to our people. I'm not talking about a city or a state. But an official apology given at the President's STATE OF THE UNION ADDRESS, where all of America shall be listening. An apology AS WELL AS LANGUAGE PRETAINING TO COMPENSATION, in the form of REPARATIONS.

RETRIBUTION is at hand. But, Retribution, we seek not for wrongs that were done. Think about that for a moment. We do seek legal compensation in the form of Reparations that legally is Owed to our people. You've stalled long enough. This is not a want. This is a historical NEED FOR THE SAKE OF THE NATION.

Europeans are the self-proclaimed saviors of the world-saviors of the un-civilized. No one asked you to come save us. And no one put a gun to your heads as in your book, John 10:10. Europeans came to "STEAL, KILL and to DESTROY" the lives of AFRICANS and native aboriginals.

You Europeans have taken full advantage of clearly, Godly people who had done you no wrong. Should Black, brown, and Red people of the earth BE APPRECIATIVE TO YOU, THE EUROPEAN race of people, FOR DOING THESE UNGODLY ACTS to the US? What manner of evil is this? That you justify, through your Christian religion, SLAVERY and the STEALING OF A PEOPLE'S LAND.

Beware of false prophets, who come to you(us) in sheep's clothing, but inwardly are ravening wolves. You are reading this, what's *your truth* in all of this? Can you and your family return to your homeland of origin? Do you and your family members speak the same language? Do your kin folk celebrate family customs and traditions? Do you have land somewhere that your great relative bequeaths to you and (or) your siblings?

What is *your truth* concerning reparations for the descendants of African and (or) Aboriginal ancestry? You do know that:

- In 1952, Germany was awarded Reparations for $ 822 million for the holocaust survivors.
- In 1971, Alaskan Natives were granted Land Settlement; $ 1 Billion plus 44 million Acres of land.
- In 1980, The Klamath of Oregon was awarded $ 81 Million.
- In 1985, The Sioux of South Dakota were awarded $ 105 Million, the Seminoles of Florida were awarded $ 12.3 Million, and the Chippewa of Wisconsin were awarded $ 31 Million.
- In 1986, The Ottawa of Michigan was awarded $ 32 million.

In 1988, Japanese Canadians were awarded $ 230 Million, and Indians\Eskimos were awarded $ 250 Million. In 1990, The Holocaust Survivors: Jewish Claim on Austria was granted $ 25 Million, and Japanese Americans were granted $ 1.2 Billion.

A precedent has been established.

Historical evidence shows and proves that none of these recipients of their reparations
- WERE FORCED TO WORK AS FREE LABORERS FOR CENTURIES as the Black and Brown people of Earth.
- None of these people of other races living in other places can claim that they BUILT UP AMERICA AS OUR ANCIENT AFRICAN ANCESTORS AND FOREFATHERS HAVE IN FACT DONE.
- ABSOLUTELY NO ONE, NO OTHER RACE OF PEOPLE ON EARTH CAN TAKE ANY SIGNIFICANT DEGREE OF CREDIT FOR BUILDING UP AMERICA as the Black and Brown melanite spirits of the earth. I CAN'T SAY THIS ENOUGH.

ALL ROADS LEAD BACK TO TRUTH....

Now, knowing what you know being true, you're wanting me and my people to simply just forget about that which occurred long ago and just ignore as you've done and just enjoy whatever crumbs you decide to throw our way? I'M HERE TO TELL YOU ALL; THAT AIN'T HAPPENING. Europeans want to convince me and my melanite brothers and sisters that due to our African ancestors and forefather's brutal and horrible treatment by the hands of your European ancestors, we, living today as descendants are not owed REPARATIONS? You're simply in denial and you're not handling TRUTH, at all. "OH, today white folks will say- I HAD NOTHING TO DO WITH SLAVERY." You're ignorant, you're an imbecile, and a Total Fool if you don't know and realize the extreme benefits you have acquired from the hundreds of years of totally, FREE LABOR THAT GENERATED A GREAT AMOUNT of wealth through currency and land ownership that was gained since the time of slavery and the stealing of native land of which you and your race of people enjoy the benefits of today.

Our people have been devastated in all manners of life, which includes economic devastation. Political devastation and educational devastation that we've had to overcome that Europeans did not have to endure. No one seems to care or think it important to address the psychological damage slavery produced that has been handed down from generation to generation and has affected both man and mankind adversely.

Dr. Joy Angela DeGruy is an author, academic, and researcher. She produced the results of her study called: POST TRAUMATIC SLAVE SYNDROME. It warrants all of humankind's intellectual and spiritual attention.

ALL ROADS LEAD BACK TO TRUTH

Words are Powerful, yet in and of themselves are useless if not attached to an action.

Until America faces truth, and its byproducts, racism, prejudice, and bigotry, people who are not of European lineage will simply continue to play an evil and bitter game of life. The game of the ILLUSION of INCLUSION. Europeans, in my opinion, are incapable of that paradigm shift (that fundamental change of approach). They are incapable of changing fundamentally, in my opinion, due to the shame that's attached to their *known recorded history*.

They don't care about repenting. If there's a Hell below, they know that they're all going to go. They've chosen to live the good life now and let what happens - happen later after their transition. Another theory is that they don't believe in their own Bible. They've simply learned to use the Bible as a manipulation tool, a controlling device over people who don't look as they do. You see, all of man and mankind needs to repent for something. Slavery, the greatest sin known to mankind, is at the top of the list that warrants the attention of repentance.

Our people have been trying, as best as they know how to intertwine themselves into the fabric of mainstream America since the early days of our freedom. The best we've achieved is pretense. Again, that illusion of inclusion. And yet White folks are the ones that are deathly afraid that we, the black, brown, and red men of the earth are going to wake up one morning and claim retribution upon all descendants of European lineage. They are afriad that we will open multiple cans of whip-ass and begin to destroy white people in the same manner that was done to our honorable ancient African ancestors, and forefathers and our native, aboriginal relatives.

SOLUTION .... SOLUTION......... SOLUTION

Black, Brown, and Red PEOPLE of the earth, the only solution to our ongoing dilemma with the European race of people is to CREATE AND MANAGE OUR OWN.

Again, we need to break away from the Europeans and their racist system and create our own. WHAT PART OF THAT DO YOU NOT UNDERSTAND?

Europeans should be ecstatic in supporting this endeavor for the Black and Brown Man to have their own in any and every conceivable manner of our imagination.

I'm not down with loving my enemies nor attempting to. I know exactly who my enemy is and have known for most of my adult life. You can continue to adhere to Martin Luther King's philosophy and ideologies concerning non-violence. If you hit me, I hit back. Whatever you violently attempt to do to me, especially if unwarranted and unprovoked, I'm doing back to you. Let's get that out of the way. Again, what part of that I've said that you don't understand? The days of our servitude and submission and turning the other cheek after being hit IS OVER WITH.

Most European's won't do shit unless with a posy to back him up. That's all the KKK was about. Running in a pack with their faces covered up. How COWARDICE was that. As a Man….as a Black man living in the 21st century, me not fighting back, as best I can, how is that scenario projecting MAN HOOD from me and to my brethren?

I know and realize that there are times that one needs to retreat, to fight another day. This ain't that time. It hasn't been that time in a very long time, for this is a different day and time. So, are you of the belief that one should die without putting up any resemblance of a fight? I probably should think that I'm going to die anyway…They're going to kill me anyway. So, just let them? That's what they do and have done to our people and the natives for a time far too long. Where's the HONOR IN DYING WITHOUT PUTTING UP A FIGHT? I'm going to be a dead nigga no matter how you look at it. If I'm to die at the hands of my oppressor for reasons they trump up as they do in most cases. It's going to be based on racism, for that's what European do and have been doing since the time of slavery.

I know and believe that I will actively and aggressively do whatever I can do as my last act on this earth which shall be to take one or more of them out with me. That is my mentality, that I will teach and promote that until my last breath. I shall take my death as an Honorable ONE. That's what "Stand your ground mean!"

A last note.... To all WHITE PEOPLE, BUT PARTICULARLY MEMBERS of law enforcement that are representative of past evil spirits of the Kul Klux Klan and Jim Crow ideologies that kill and brutally torment Black, Brown, and Red men of the earth unjustly and without cause, merit, or justification,,,,,,,

I believe that YOUR RETRIBUTION SHALL BE AT HAND AS WELL. WHAT GOES AROUND SHALL COME AROUND.... TEN-FOLD, BACK TO YOU AND YOUR FAMILY MEMBERS. I BELIEVE THAT SOME ONE OR SOME GROUP WILL TAKE IT UPON THEMSELVES - VIGILANTY JUSTICE TO YOU AND ALL the devils THAT has DECIDED TO BE THE SELF-PROCLAIMED JUDGE, JUROR, AND EXECUTIONER.

Your reconning shall be upon you. AND MAY GOD NOT HAVE MERCY ON YOUR SOULS.

MA 'at\Hotep

Ase

Solution: Separation

For those who allow themselves to think outside the box, who dare to dream, who are fed up with America's hypocrisy, separation is our only viable, intelligent option to keep.

Separating from the Europeans may in fact be the most difficult proposition to do for most of our people.
It too is doable.

However, Native / Aboriginals are examples we can learn from.
The ugly reality is that, psychologically, we have been conditioned to depend upon the European for almost everything. We've had to get their permission to do, or to be, during most of our stay, here in America.

Thus, it's out of most of our people's comprehension, in the idea of creating our own realities, living on our own, autonomous lands. Not being under the Europeans foot, pressing on our collective necks, not being under their jurisdiction, nor rules of their racist, administrations of their laws.

I'm not suggesting that we leave American soil, for our ancestors, and forefathers has paid the ultimate price for present day black folk to be here. Our ancestor's blood permeates the soil of America. Our Ancestors and forebears-built America. Our people are not immigrants. We are legally authorized and rightfully bound to be here compared to all others. For the extremist, hateful to the core, white people, that has never desired blacks, and whites to co-mingle, nor to be integrated, who's sentiment has always been that of, "go back to Africa". You should be the first to give an Amen and vote Yes to the idea of separation.

My proposal in separating from the Europeans is as follows:

America can be cut up into 3 territories.

The white race, and all those who want to be viewed as white, you all should jump for joy. Due to you all's physical characteristics, and your natural inclination for / suited for the cold climate, should be awarded the northern / northwestern portion of America. The only occupants within this territory, (unless approved by the white race), shall be that of European lineage.

White people

- White people would no longer have to pretend that you genuinely mean black folks any good.
- White people won't have pretend to like black folks any longer.
- White folks won't have to pretend to enjoy black folks' company.
- White people, forever, no longer have to pretend to trust black folks.
- White people will no longer have to pretend not to be fearful of black folks, and our potential, retaliatory uprising which could occur at any moment in time.
- White Klan members wold NOT have to pretend that they like and support thier females co-habitating/marrying black flesh.

Black people

Our people, who have been fed up, for a very, very long time, who are believers that America will get worse, before it gets better, who have become exacerbated with that notion, who are fed up with America's hypocrisy, due to our physical characteristics, that are more inclined / suited for the warmer climate, should be awarded the southern / southeastern portion of America.

> The only occupants within our territory, (unless, approved by the Elders), shall be that of African, and (or) Aboriginal lineage.
> Black folks will no longer, have to pretend to genuinely like, nor enjoy Europeans company.
> Black folks will no longer have to pretend that we trust the white man, on any level.
> Black folks will no longer have to pretend that we truly respect the white man, just because they are white.
> Black folks will no longer have to pretend that we accept, continually living in hell on earth, particularly here in America, co – habituating among white people.

And, black folks, theoretically, won't have to depend on the white man for life essentials .

There should exist a neutral territory / portion of the new America.

From a portion of the European's North, from a portion from the melanated South, (Middle / Neutral territory), that should separate the two, but where the continuation of business as usual, can exist, among those who desire to co-mingle.

Of course, this is merely, a rough estimate of an idea. Has anyone of you thought of anything similar? Like Iseral and Palestine.

To those that the idea of separating resonates remotely within your spirits and intellect, who would choose and even desire the opportunity to be a part of creating a new America, where no one has to pretend, where the whites race has to fight to keep, or the black race has to fight to acquire. Where both have access to neutrality (business as usual), within the neutral territory.

Black people's, new humanitarian society, based on spirituality, opposite and separate from the systemic, raciest society we've ever known, know and believe - that it too is doable.
If we can see it / we can do it. If we can imagine it / we can bring it into existence.

To all melenated beings, know this; you should not desire to be part of, or come to the new society if you're bringing the baggage of the European's virus. If you have not recognized that you're infected by their European virus, you do not need to desire, nor consider coming to the new black society.

Stay in the neutral zone, and continue to live out your life in an environment you've only known. It shall not be an automatic conclusion that you, nor I will qualify to be accepted. That is the decision of the Elders, who I believe should be the final authority, concerning all matters related to the New Society.

One should know and believe that one's behavior, and beliefs should be representative of the antidotal affects towards counteracting their virus, as well as the qualifying to live in the new society.

It makes absolutely no sense what -so-ever to bring America's hypocrisy, corrupt capitalistic system, criminal elements, including all facets of corruption, into our new reality. Nor should you bring their white, created Jesus. It makes absolutely no sense whatever to duplicate what we've been forcefed for the past 400+ years in this New Society

AGAIN...

Allow me to state unequivocally that just as abolitionist existed back in the day, presently there does exist good, decent God fearing, humanitarian white folks. Unfortunately, there is simply not enough of you, to make a difference. Nor are you in positions to create policies, rules, laws, or regulations. *European Bullies out number you.*

Present day Europeans are truly worst beings, then that of their predecessors. Why? Because, white folks of today, collectively have chosen to continually perpetuate, and

benefit from that which they feel so uncomfortable about
…Their despicable history.

-That history that they don't want their children to feel
ashamed of.
-That history that whites' folks today are trying to hide.
-That same ugly history that presents day whites have not
attempted to correct, by making whole a people that their
kind put into bondage.
-Yes, it shall also, forever reflect to the European's children,
and that of generations to come, their parent's, relatives,
friends, and associates, true moral character among their
white race.
-The European's character, and those same children, and
their children, and their children's character, shall forever
be on trial .
- Always re-writing the same narrative, over, and over, and
over, until America is no more.
That type of history cannot / will not, ever, simply
disappear.
-In fact, it shall forever be enhanced, and unable to delete
itself from the minds of both Man, and Mankind .
-And, it's all due to Europeans perpetuating their ancestors
wrongs, even though they all are more educated, and
better informed .

 Europeans and all others who agree with the continuation
of the self-inflicted insanity you've created and has
maintained for over 400 years, you shall reap what you
have sowed.
 You cannot undo the past, but looking toward the future,
you can begin the healing process, right at this very

moment, for yourselves as well as for the people you've mistreated.

I ask myself, "are you, as the white race of people, collectively capable in transcending into exhibiting the moral values that your founding fathers wrote on paper? If history being the barometer, indicator, = I think not.

To my people, most of us do wear the cloak of denial.
Our collective denial of being Europeanized.
Our collective denial that exists within the psyche of our people, that prompts one to be against, hurt and kill another who looks like themselves, triggered by America's systemic, racism.

That denial that our people has been breaded to be divisive to a fault.
Our abilities to come together, to unify, to confront the life and death issues of Our people have been compromised.
  We've been programed not to trust one another.
  We exist every day in our juices of denial by rejecting the notion as well as the in-your-face realities that this America isn't meant for us due to the way it was constructed, and the methods used to gain superiority over our people.
  Our collective denial that their religious beliefs coincide with our natural, eternal spirituality.
  Our collective denial towards not knowing nor believing that we can do and be without the European's input nor permission.
  Our collective denial that we're unable to create our own realities by separating from the Europeans and formulating our own spiritual based society, within our own sovereign lands.

Easier said than done, I know. But it's our only recourse.

-The Europeans has illegally obtained what they have, thus in their minds, believe that they have the right to do as they see fit.

Europeans can care less of the notion of levelling the playing field.

-They can care less of the notion of rejecting the historical non-truths that they've perpetrated for over 400 + years.

-They can care less of engaging the psychoanalysis of their own people towards aiming to release pent-up or repressed emotions and memories to treat the mental conditions of their conscious and unconscious elements in their minds.

They can care less in relinquishing any degree of perceived power.

-Europeans can care less that reparations are a healing mechanism, that can propel healing to all of America, and its citizens.

-For the European, it appears to be too painful an ordeal, too painful of a journey to bring what existed and what presently exist at their unconscious or subconscious levels, up to their consciousness and deal honorably with their misdeeds as a people.

-Europeans can care less in their ability to do so, for it could possibly be their beginning towards their needed healing process. The healing that's so desperately needed for the betterment for all of Man and Mankind.

So, my people, stop bitching and complaining that they treat you and me unfairly.

You and I know exactly what time it is and has always been.

For those who choose to stay in residence of what was taught to them at an early age, who denies the truths, facts, and evidence of historical proportions, who's only recourse is to simply pretend to enjoy the illusion of inclusion,,,

Pretending that prayer without works and continue to say to the universe that you have hope and possess the amount of faith that is the size of a mustard seed, that God will resolve your issues concerning both sides of the equation.

There exist no words created that will break the chain of your conservative, mental bondage of denial.

Being and choosing to stay in self-Denial shall forever be your permanent residence.

Faith without works is dead which speaks volumes concerning our realities co- existing alongside our oppressors.

If you choose to do nothing, nothing shall be done.

Words are powerful, yet in and of themselves are useless if not attached to an action …

Separation is of course not a new phenomenon of thought.

Europeans at this present time in history are exploring the possibility of colonizing space, of all places.

They are looking to separate themselves from us, and this America, that they themselves created,

as well as the planet earth.

There exists no other pressing topic that warrants our immediate attention regarding the evolution of OUR people.

If we allow continually, our evolution shall always be blocked, in some way, shape, form, or fashion by white people.

Can we do without them?   Hell yes.
Can they do without Us?   Personally, I don 't thinks so.
Europeans, due to their created history, seem to need to have their foot on our people necks. Who will they have at their disposal to abuse, outside of people of color?

 Don't talk about it / be about it.
I, for one, says, I'm not from Missouri, but - Show me -, Europeans, that you can do without black meat …Brown flesh …myelinated beings in this America you've created.

Our Spiritual connection with our Creator / Power source, and the fight that most of us should be engaged in, towards the acquisition of collecting an historical debt that have been owed for centuries, appears to be inconspicuous to the Europeans as well as to our own people roaming this land called America.

This is an honorable endeavor that shall come around once in a lifetime for us who are still here.

As for my one vote, I vote yes, for both reparations, as well as separation.
 I am personally motivated in this fight.
My motivation is directly geared towards Recognizing, and Honoring OUR Ancient Ancestors, OUR NOT TOO LONG AGO FOREFATHERS, ELDERS, PRESENT DAY

BEINGS, as well as for Our FUTURE GENERATIONS that is to follow .

Our victory in Creating Our Own Reality should produce a dignified, ceremonial event, for All the Universe to marvel, (something that causes wonder, admiration, or astonishment; a WONDERFUL THING).

Our Ancestors, Forefathers, and We of present day, are Certified, Qualified, and shall exemplify Righteously, the Honor, and Unadulterated Respect that's due, Morally, and legally, to the DESERVERS,
            even If You are not.

And If Not Now /// WHEN???????

     I am not an historian.
     I have not obtained any educational degree from a college nor university.
     I have no distinct rank, nor do I possess any special attributes nor qualifications.
     I am not considered a professional writer, by any means, (as you can obviously tell).

     Who am I?

I am a common man, living off modest means.
.
 I'm 68, soon to be 69 years young.
I am an Elder.

I've had my run-ins with the law.
I am opinionated.

I am a fleshly, living being that know and believes that I've listened to my inner spirit as of late, even if I've been stubborn in the past in doing so.

I've been instructed to tell all those stubborn, (young and old), spirits like me, that you should tell your story or a story.
That you are a professional storyteller when it comes to expressing that which lies within.
As I, you may not have the technical aspects down for writing, or even know of their existence, but, if writing ain 't your thing, then speak your truths into a recording device, of your choice.
You are still the director, the editor, as well as the headliner performer, regurgitating your reality.
And if you are internally motivated to tell the world of your personal ideas / opinions, then do so, while you can.
Tomorrow is not promised, to none of us. Today could be your last. Tomorrow can be your new beginning.
Leave something behind, other than a memory.

No different than the movies, and tv shows that you've become addicted to.
Listening and watching religiously, that stems from another 's imagination.
There's no right nor wrong telling your story or a story.
"Therefore, if anyone is in the Creator, the New creation has come; The old has gone, the new is here."
I 've presented my analysis, of the European.

Note: I 've presented my analysis, of my People.

I 've presented my solutions to all of MAN, and MANKIND.

Before you criticize me, for whatever reason(s), what is your Analysis? What are your solutions towards eradicating presentd-day racism in America?

Have you had any resemblance in thought, towards my offered solutions?

If you have, then, I'm not alone.
If you haven't, then meditate, and see what you come up with.

Tell your story, or a story, that may resonate within someone else spirit. Speak your trues. One 's trues, are as relevant as any other. Even the racist. Even the house N's. Believe and know that – to be a Fact.

Alafia

As – salamu alaykum   Hotep / Ase'

--Ase' --

P. S.   A reminder: In white America, the fact that black, brown, and myelinated people have had to fight for human rights since America's inception, rights that others are extended at birth, is an obvious, crystal-clear indictment as well as an indicator, of the racial divisiveness that has always existed. Any rational, thinking being, even if they are considered legally blind - can see the disparity.

Caucasians / Europeans / white people will response to my essay, (in most cases), as non – truths. Facts, that's married to Truth … they will naturally, predictably disagree. It's in their DNA to do so. Many of my people will also disagree. More likely than not, they are the very ones that is in: Absolute, total Denial.

RESPECT the message, if not the messenger!

Reparations

Intrinsically, Long Overdue

I begin this portion of my book, by acknowledging two Brothers, (from another mother). They are my mentors. They both have assisted me towards my development, gravitating me towards conscious thought, and awareness .

They alone, have introduced me to my own history, and knowledge pertaining to our people's original spiritual concepts.

> Brothers, Elder Horace Canty, and
> Brother Clifton Williams Jr.
> Thank you both…

Hotep / MA 'at

--*Ase'* --

Now, let's begin …

The Enemy that Lurks Within Reparations

Our journey now begins with knowing and believing that there will be an anticipated battle, an anticipated fight with the European and their government.

We know that there will be casualties along the way during our Honorable quest for legally owed Reparations for the

Black and Brown people of America and possibly around the world.

But our more profound battle and fight will not be with the European, but rather with THE ENEMY THAT LURKS WITHIN our individual and collective spirits as a race of people.

I am reminded of the song, "Smiling Faces ", sung by" The Undisputed Truth ".

Know and believe, there exist among our people, traitors. Traitors who are going to present themselves to you and me with smiling faces, pretending to be your / our friend, showing no traces of the evil that lurks within.
The word Traitor is defined as, "one who betrays another's trust or is false to an obligation or duty".

For those of righteousness, who understand the obligation to duty towards the Honoring of our ancestors through the acquisition of Reparations, our number one adversarial component will be that of people who shall look as you do.

As the song suggests, sometimes, they won't tell you the truth. They will tell lies, and eventually, you will obtain proof.

The truth shall be in their eyes, cause the eyes don't lie. The song reminds one to be aware of the handshake, that hides the snake, (can u dig it?).

You / I should be aware of the pat on the back, for it just might hold you / myself back.

Spurned by jealousy, misery, envy, often, one cannot see behind smiling faces that don't tell the truth.

Our enemy, and oppressor won't do us any harm, in that we already know where they are coming from. Don't let the handshake and smile fool you ...take the advice, I'm only tryin' to school ya.

Smiling faces, smiling faces, sometimes – they don't tell the truth.

Smiling faces show no traces of the evil that lurks within.

BEWARE

--*Alse'*--

Reparations is in fact, long overdue to our people.

I've said this before.
I am not a historian, nor do I possess any degree from a college, nor university.
I hold no distinct rank, nor position.
I do not possess any medals of valor, nor special attributes.
This writing is for me, representing my contribution to all of Man, and Mankind, that stems from my spirit.
I present to you my dissertation:
"A common man's Perspective on the subject of REPARATIONS, for the black population of America."

- Let's Ride -

I am of the opinion, that there exist No Greater issue, that is worthy, than that of acquiring Reparations for us, who are of African, and (or), Aboriginal linage, residing, Specifically, in America, as well as abroad.

Due to world history, and specifically, that which resides in the annals of American history, the black, brown, and myelinated race of people are urgently Owed Reparations, from this – United States government, the catholic church, wealthy banking families, and all other entities that have benefited, since the time OUR PEOPLE WERE INSLAVED... up to present day.

Let us pray:

Most Honorable, Magnificent, Creator,

the One, or They, who are thought to be Omnipotent, concerning that of all things,
 We ceremonially, come before Thee - in Joyful Prayer.
 For, it is through Prayer that we communicate with Thee, and beseech solemn request for help, or expressions of Thanks.

Creator, The Deity above all others, Thou who have brought all things into existence, we profoundly Acknowledge Thee, as Our Power Source, for it is through thy spiritual powers, that corrects our voltage, current, and frequency, concerning life matters, of extreme importance.

We come before Thee, not to ask, nor beg for Anything, for Thou has Already given, and provided, already, everything to both, Man, and Mankind, that we could ever hope for, or imagine.

We, who are your earthly vessels, who are commanded, through words, and deeds of expressions, that of Your Devine Will.
Yet, Omnipotent Creator, today, there exist a serious discrepancy, concerning the question, what is Your Devine Will for both Man, and Mankind?

 It is this sanctified question Creator, that both Man and Mankind appear to be perplexed, in regard of the application, concerning Your Devine Will.

Our heavenly Power Source, I, and others, submit a solemn request for Help from Thee.
We all need Your Divine intervention, concerning the revelation of meaning of Your Devine Will.

There are those among the living, who thinks they know you. They, who are affiliated with various denominations of administrative structure, characterized by their doctrines, and practices, adhere to being greater, and healthier, than any other prescribed direction of remedy of salvation, and redemption.
That their religious, ideologies of beliefs in their worship, supersede that of anyone else's.
Even more importantly Honorable Creator, there exist various religions that believe that their actions of choice, regarding their behavior, towards a race of people, that their interpretation of their exemplification of what Righteousness looks like, are profoundly undisputable.

Help us Beings, that of human, belonging to that of Man, help us, thy supreme authority, to decipher, right, from wrong, / good, from evil.

Help us to finally see, clearly, that which is noble, in thine eyes.

We call upon Your Devine assistance in decoding the essence of You.

We ask of You, to direct all servants of You, directing Our collective steps, in confirmation, representative of Your Goodness, over that, which is evil.

Thou know what lies deepest in the four corners of our hearts, souls, minds, and spirits.

Thou know our inter most thoughts, even before we know our own. We reach out to You, right now, for Your Devine mercy, guidance, and understanding.

Through our calling, we ask that You EDIFY Our collective Hearts, Minds, Bodies, and Souls, through our individual, as well as collective Spirits.

We are all in desperate need of Your spiritual edification.

Your edification toward our enlightenment, of instruction of improvement, especially in moral, and spiritual matters.

Touch us, oh Righteous one, here, right now, in the manner, that we all need to be touched. Bless us, Almighty Creator, right now, in the manner, that we need to be blessed.

Assist us, through spiritual means, to find the strength within ourselves, to lift ourselves up, as a people, from the bowels of despair, existing in this racist democracy, this dangerous land, we call America.

We need thee.
We need Thee, right now, for our own sake.
We need thy presence, to reveal thy self, within each one of us.

Allow Your Holiness of spirit, to collectively, sit in council of collaboration, of both Man, and Mankind. At this juncture, we all just want to say THANK YOU. THANK YOU. THANK YOU.

Thank you almighty for allowing the living, to see, and experience the day gone by.

We thank Thee, for protecting those of us, from all hurt, harm, and danger, during the day, during our travels, and interactions with others.

We Thank Thee in anticipation of night, as we prepare to receive the blessings of restful sleep.

We thank Thee, in anticipation for the sunrise of tomorrow.

We thank Thee also, for the knowledge of the Divine attributes of the Forces of Nature.

We Thank Thee, whole heartily, for the appreciation of the knowledge, that of possessing, and administering, that of Free Will.

We Thank Thee for the progression of Your Spirit.

We Thank Thee for the divinity that You've offered to both, Man, and Mankind.

We thank Thee in all things.

We, who are not worthy, collectively, THANK YOU in advance, for Your Supreme BLESSINGS, of the gift of life.

We simply can Never Thank You enough, for the Spiritual Nourishment that You provide.

We Humbly, and with all Humility, thank Thee, here, and now, for allowing us the opportunity, and privilege to converse with Thee.

NOW, as the Power vested in me, a common man's spirit, I decree, that the manifestation of Your Divine Will, shall be done, here on earth … as it is, and shall be bequeath unto both, Man, and Mankind, the revelation of Humanity, bosomed with that of All Righteousness, which shall be administered,

through Thy Devine Spirit, on America's soil, and throughout the Universe.
For, together We Shall Stand, ,,,,,,,,,,Divided, We Shall surely, inevitably Fall.
Calling upon Your Holy name ...
Praise be unto the HIGHEST...
Through Our Honorable Ancestors, we
pray.

Maat / Hotep

--*Ase'*--

Criterion for Reparations

The definition for Reparations is: the making of amends for a wrong one has done, by paying money to, or otherwise helping those who have been wrong.

According to the United Nations: Adequate, effective, and prompt reparations is intended to promote justice by redressing gross violations of international human rights law or serious violations of International humanitarian law.

Unfulfilled promise ...
There have been much said, in recent times about reparations. Allow me to be blunt, and to the point. On January 16, 1865, the U. S. government, by way of Union General William T. Sherman 's special order number 15,

Promised, to the soon to be freed slaves, 40 acres and a mule, (the mule was to come later). The U. S. government HAS NEVER made good on that promise.

Published, Wednesday, August, 12, 2020 / Updated Monday, August, 17, 2020, William Darity, professor of public policy at Duke University, have studied the rationale, and design of reparations for more than 30 years. He says, "the present moment seems to afford more of an opportunity to move forward than any moment I've experienced in my lifetime."

Darity, and his wife, Kirsten Mullen, made the most comprehensive case for a reparations program in their latest book", From Here to Equality ".Reparations for Black Americans, in the "Twenty – First Century".

They argue, a meaningful program to eliminate the existing Black – White wealth gap requires an allocation of between $ 10 trillion, and $ 12, trillion, or about $ 800,000 to EACH eligible Black household. But not everyone agrees that now is the time to pay reparations.

You tell me, when is the time to pay our people reparations? And, why haven 't the U. S. government, the catholic church, and the wealthy banking families, (and all entities that have benefited), paid reparations, back when it was cheaper to do so?

When the payout would have been around a grand, or two. Or when it was around a hundred grand ? They chose not to pay when it was cheaper to do so, because, in my opinion, they have no intentions to ever pay, that which is legally, and morally proper to do so.

Their intentions aside, it is totally Our responsibility, collectively, as a race of people, to force their hand, and hold them accountable for the Outstanding debt that is intrinsically Owed.

I, for one have asked myself, who got America in so much debt in the first place?

I answered myself by saying, "Self, why should I care about America 's debt?

And I ask myself this question, primarily, due to the fact, that I realized that it is exclusively, the Europeans who are responsible, who have accumulated this stupid / asinine amount of debt, that is directly, (in my opinion), due to the European ' s greed, corruption , and their thirst for supreme, worldly power .

The Europeans, the white man, Caucasians, whom originated from the Caucasoid mountains, (cave dwellers), are directly responsible for the financial hole America finds its self in .

There have been 46 presidencies, (Only ONE BLACK president), and 45 people have served as president. So, by my arithmetic, 45 presidents have been that of the European clan.

So, again, why in heaven's name should I, or for that matter, Any Black person, who is of Truth, and Facts, who are of consciousness, give a Damn about America ' s debt situation ?

As far as I 'm concerned, these sequences of events, concerning America 's debt, have been diabolically, designed on purpose.

Europeans / America 's government have absolutely no intentions on paying off America 's debt, to whomever is owed. PERIOD. As an American citizen, this is the way I see this situation, and I 'm sticking to it ...

Who else are the American citizens to blame?
Who else should be held accountable? Surely, not the Black, brown, myelinated beings existing in America.

NOW, they can, and will ALWAYS use this as their primary reason, or excuse towards not Honoring the Promise, given in the year of 1865.

The Europeans, the catholic church, the wealthy banking families, (the Rockefellers, the Rothschilds, Ovia, and the Peruzzi), and all entities thereof, that have benefited from the time of Our Ancestors enslavement ,and Our forefathers era of Jim Crow, Owe our people, with interest, for over the past 158 years.

If You, or I owed the IRS, (the government), as an example, any amount of money, they will present to You, and I, (on the quick), payment options, that shall include = full payment, short – term payment, (paying in 180 days or less), or a long – term payment plan, (installment agreement) ,(paying monthly).

So, if not now – When, takes on a whole new meaning for them, as well as for Our people.
It is time, and the time is Now, for Our people to receive, that which is rightfully Ours to claim.

It's time for the overdue payment, for the insurmountable wrongs that have been perpetrated upon a people, that have Never deserved the harsh realities of the inhumanity the Europeans placed upon.

Evidence

Evidence is an intricate element in supporting Our case for reparations.

For clarification, evidence is defined as: the available body of facts or information indicating whether a brief or proposition is true, and valid.

I 've uncovered approximately 77 different types of evidence criterion.

Some examples include = Admissible evidence.

Clear, and convincing evidence.

Credible evidence.

Conclusive evidence.

Documentary evidence.

And Historical evidence, and others.

Precedent

Another crucial, and critical element that is necessary in validating the call for reparations is Precedent.

Precedent is defined as: in common law legal systems – a precedent or authority is a legal case that establishes a principal or rule. This principle, or rule is then used by the court or other judicial bodies use when deciding later cases with … similar issues or facts.

Let's now examine similar events, and issues of facts, in which reparations were granted unto victimized groups of people of other races, in other places: 1952, Germany is awarded reparations in the amount of $ 822 million for Holocaust survivors.

1971, Alaskan natives are granted Land Settlement; $ 1 Billion plus 44 million acres of land.

1980, The Klamath, (native), of Oregon are awarded $ 81 million.

1985, The Sioux (native), of South Dakota are awarded $ 105 million.

The Seminoles of Florida are awarded $ 12.3 million, and the Chippewa of Wisconsin are awarded $ 31 million.

1986, The Ottawas of Michigan were awarded $ 32 million.

1988, Japanese Canadians are awarded $ 230 million.

Eskimos are awarded 250,000mi.2

1990, The holocaust survivors 'Jewish claim on Austria is granted $ 25 million, Japanese Americans are awarded $ 1.2 Billion.

Ladies, and gentlemen, it is my humble opinion that the provided information does in fact, legally, establishes Precedent.

This information of facts also shows within the historical evidence, that NONE of the previously – mentioned recipients were forced to work as, "FREE LABORERS", for hundreds of years like Our African Ancestors/

forefathers and resent relatives were. Thus, they shall not be credited, to any respectable degree as for participating in the building / construction of this America. Our people-built America ...PERIOD.

Most Crucial / Important Ingredient, towards the acquisition, of said reparations,

Is Y O U...the PEOPLE?

The acquisition of reparations is a NEED, not a want.
It's needed for the Black families.
It's needed for the Black communities / neighborhoods.
It's needed for the development of OUR culture.
Its needed, for our people's, deplorable, economic status.
The fruits from the acquisition of reparations shall be substantial, in a great number of ways.

In closing:
Collectively, we have a common foe.
To those of us that possess some degree of pride in being black, and to those of us that have reached, or is trying to reach a higher level of consciousness, We Must put aside our petty individual differences, galvanize our collective selves on all levels, in all things .
We, as a body of people, must direct ourselves, and our collective spirits towards the totality of purpose.

The acquisition, of   Reparations - shall be Life changing for us all.

?   ?   ?   If not Now ... WHEN? ? ?   ?

?
?   ?   ?   ?   ?   ?

Who is to Pay for Past Crimes for Slavery's Atrocities?

Who is to be Held Accountable for present day crimes of racial Unlawfulness?
Words are Powerful, yet in and of themselves are useless if not attached to an action…

The Actions of Crimes that occurred in the past which are considered heinous by today's standards of American society have no statute of limitations. There is no statute of limitations for kidnapping, first degree murder, rape, sexual assault upon an adult or child. Brutal hangings, burnings of human flesh and malicious castrations, which is the intentional maiming of another person's genitalia. Then considered common law offenses, are representative of crimes of atrocities that have yet to be resolved nor prosecuted.

Discriminatory applications of European's laws then that was placed upon a people who were kidnaped from their homeland (s) exist today. Cases involving severe crimes like these typically have no maximum period of limitations. You tell me, who is to pay for the historically documented Atrocities that occurred on American soil upon the Africans and the Indigenous of whom the Black, Brown, and Red man of earth living present day (myelinated people) who we are direct descendants of?   Example: Germans and Jews …

The first international war crimes tribunal in history revealed the true extent of German atrocities against a race of people that were recognized as Jews and held some of the most prominent Nazis accountable for their crimes.

The atrocity of Slavery is and has already been revealed. The documented history of America cries out to be substantiated and redeemed. America needs to cleanse itself through a similar war crime international tribunal. Retribution is at hand. Retribution is standing directly in front of the government and its citizens of America.

European citizens living today, young, and old as well as the projected future generations to come are officially not responsible for those crimes of inhumanity that their ancestors and founding fathers executed through their chosen Actions of the past. But also let it be known and let it be said that throughout the world the Europeans and subsequently all others who have embraced the European's ideologies of life subsequently benefit meaningfully, significantly as well as fundamentally in today's America in all conceivable manner of commerce due to those exact heinous crimes that their ancestors perpetrated upon a people who did not ask to be kidnapped nor to be enslaved.

Our honorable ancestors did not voluntarily choose to be inhumanely treated for the purpose towards the buildup of America from the ground floor for the invaders and enslavers selfish need for power by way of subjective and intentional abusive forced labor. Europeans and all other immigrants simply choose to ignore and deflect historical facts that they just do not want to deal with.

The unmitigated TRUTH that stems from Christopher Columbus's arrival upon native's land that set-in motion the European's inaugural beginning has false narratives and has no meaningful concern of consequence for the Europeans. Also known as Caucasians, Europeans purposefully and intentionally ignore the facts pertaining to the unlawful misdeeds of inhumanity of the past.

Today as then, myelinated beings live in a racially combustible, money driven, racist systemic environment every day of our lives. All beings that are not of European lineage are in the crosshairs of authority. Those entities of authority that our people are often without cause nor provocation can be subjected to blatant racism as American citizens while living here on American soil. Myelinated beings are consistently presented in all facets of life as a prerequisite of provoked acceptance that we are to view as normal behavior from our oppressors. Primarily, the European race of people has literally destroyed millions of Black, Brown, and Red man lives and their families. Myelinated people suffered back in the day as well as present day. Black folks receive no empathy from being treated disrespectfully.

What are we as myelinated American citizens to do? Are we as Myelinated people to do Nothing in Honoring those spirits that were Kidnapped from their homeland? Was that action not a crime in and of itself? Was it not a crime that human beings were transported in the hulls of slave ships, shackled and Chang, packed like sardines in a can? Existing and living in their own vomit and feces, their lives discarded at the whim and will of their enslavers.

Was it not a crime to be brutally treated, human flesh whipped as if it were a four-legged animal? Was it not a crime of inhumanity to be forced to work from sunup to sundown? Was it not a crime to be forced into NOT being compensated Monetarily or by the acquisition of Land for one 's labor? Was it not a crime to be murdered, raped, sodomized, castrated, burned, hung, including ALL OTHER MANNERS one can possibly imagine that would be today considered Atrocities of INHUMANITY?

Isn't it ironic that our awareness of knowledge comes directly from the very people that perpetrated these known atrocities upon a people that we are direct descendants of? But the Europeans feel no obligation to amend that of their ancestors' wrong doings. Why? Why are the Europeans so adamant toward Not apologizing on behalf of their Ancient Ancestors and founding fathers cruel and unusual punishment towards the African and Natives who were here on this land before they were? If any one of us today, (particularly if these crimes were applied from a person not of European decent) committed any of these atrocities, the authorities would kill us on the spot or place us in prison and throw away the keys for our remaining natural lives... PERIOD. No questions asked.

Hence, the racial disparity existing presently in America. And why are we / why should we as a people continually today be ostracized, condemned, and persecuted for existing? Please, do not form your mouths to say that myelinated people are Not treated as being ostracized, condemned nor persecuted daily living here in America. If you do, that will indicate once again that you (as an individual) are choosing to speak with a forked tongue. We as a people have attempted to conform to your ideologies pertaining to life in general. Many of our people has tried to duplicate as well as imitate your appearance in dress, mannerisms, speech and more importantly, many of us has been force fed in believing in accepting your God. Yet, our actions have not been received collectively by the European race of people as not enough for us to be accepted as rightfully, equal citizens residing side by side.

Due to our Ancestors, we are qualified, certified, and legally authorized to live here in America than any immigrants, including you, (the European race of people). As a people, we know and believe (internally) that it should and shall be mandatory for us to honorably seek and pursue ways and methods in Honoring our deceased Ancestors, as well as our realization of realism in considering separating ourselves from your reluctance in treating our people in the manner you yourselves would want and desire to be treated. There are those among us that have seen and experienced enough. There are those among us who are tired of being tired living in an environment of systemic racism. Collectively, we as a people are simply tired of being tired of the unprovoked aggression that follows all of us at any moment of time. No amount of money nor status exempts our people from potential death nor injuries from white citizens as well as agents of the law that are supposed to be protectors and servers of all citizens living and residing on American soil. All negativity that follows our people has been learned from you, the Europeans.

AMERICA … considered the most powerful Nation on earth, yet on the verge of self-destruction. Self-destruction due to the INTERNAL STRIFE that permeates unconditionally throughout its borders. You define "internal strife" as: an insurgency that encompasses a range of situations from peaceful to violent protests and demonstrations to rebellions against the government to full- blown armed conflicts. Myelinated people view Europeans generally as uncompromising. Due to this perceived stance, in my opinion, does it constitute our need for restoration and restitution?

Restoration: the action of returning something to a former owner, place, or condition. Can we say that we, as a people, need to be returned is our collective dignity? Can we say that we need our 40 acres and a mule? Can we say that we need to be returned to our natural condition of existence? Can we say and agree that as a people – we need to be returned to our place of origin.

It is a known fact that Europeans cannot return our people back to our original place (s) of origin for that task shall be impossible, absurd, futile, inconceivable to achieve nor accomplish. Our Ancestors were indeed the former owners of a place and their condition.

Restitution: is the restoration of something lost or stolen to its proper owner. We as a people have been lost living among Europeans. Our people have been deprived in the natural sense of our Ancestors 's rituals, customs, languages, deity, appearances, and all other learned developmental agencies of growth that was stolen, taken away, beaten out of ... decades ago.

History frames both man and mankind's present condition (s). America and its citizens have made it perfectly clear that America will stubbornly continue to choose Not to create greatness for / in America.

Note: I did not say "in making America great again", for from the eyes of black and brown people, America has never been considered great. Myelinated occupants living the Illusion of Inclusion, in essence forever - cannot - and shall not constitute greatness by any stretch of one 's imagination.

Europeans sees America as being great obviously from their perspective for their enslaving of a people that built America and the thievery that followed, deceitfully and violently taking land from the indigenous natives. Hold your roll... do not get upset nor angry of the TRUTH. TRUTH is TRUTH, like it or not. So, tell me white people, what shall be your collective ulterior motives in depriving our people our right of need to be free of you and your dominance over our collective lives? Think about that for a moment ... Black and Brown citizens of America seek the uplifting of our people – not through violence, but through moral and legal means. Europeans always desire and like to hear words pertaining to non – violence. Isn't that a blimp ...The pot calling the kettle black?

Europeans HAS ALWAYS BE THE ENTITY that has used violence to achieve all that they 've acquired. Still today,

Europeans brings violence to our collective doorsteps, killing us over broken taillights, car registration papers, for jogging in white neighborhoods, for selling cigarettes on the street. Law enforcement breaking doors down, entering the wrong house, killing, and injuring the occupants, with absolutely no adjudication upon the zealous officers involved. Black and brown folks being falsely accused by white women as being the perpetrator of a crime that did not even exist. Our people being killed over meaningless perceived infractions. White people committing mass murders taken alive, to have their day in court.

It is simply a travesty, a declaration of sort toward our treatment living in racist white America. While America 's judicial system (in most cases) defines and supports their actions. All this injustice, justified in most cases by Europeans and sell outs. The bearers of violence again have ALWAYS been that of the Europeans, not of black folks. We may self-inflict violence upon ourselves, but I know that it is primarily due to the conditions that our people have been forced into. Violence is forever present towards myelinated spirits living in America, motivated by evil forces.

Who qualifies to be compensated morally and legally for the past and present-day unlawful atrocities of inhumanities? Answer: Myelinated beings of lineage of African and (or) Aboriginal decent shall be the qualifiers of compensations due to the past of those who no longer are living, who were the actual receptors who suffered the wrongs and misdeeds who no longer lives above ground. We today qualify for modern day misdeeds of racial injustice. Other races living in other places as well as those living on American soil that have legally qualified and received compensatory (intended to recompense someone who has experienced loss, suffering, or injury) reward from past wrongs and misdeeds of inhumanity due to their connection of lineage.

I beg to ask the ultimate question:
Who or what guilty party (parties) are legally and morally responsible for the unthinkable injustices that has been documented in America 's archives, storytelling in all mediums including that of movies, books and any other form of educational / entertainment disseminating of information, exposing those atrocities upon myelinated people throughout America, s history?   That of the past as well as present day crimes of disparities has in most cases no Legal nor Moral statute of limitation that is directly reflective of the European's own established laws?

What manner of entity is to be held as the primary defendants responsible for the atrocities of past misdeeds is the question? In conjunction, who are the co – defendants that are and should be attached and held accountable for the insanity and chaos created by the Europeans, that is saturated in the ongoing conspiracies that has existed for centuries? Who are we, (the myelinated people of earth) to charge and hold accountable for the international, universal, and intentional crimes of Inhumanity upon Our Ancient African Ancestors and our Indigenous relatives?

In my humble opinion, we are to hold the Pontiff (s), the official leader (s) of the Catholic church.

We are to hold the newly formed U.S. GOVERNMENT liable as being a Primary defendant in this matter. Included are their co - defendants who are without question, those prestigious banking families, and their subsidiaries. Inclusive also shall be all entities of business and commerce that have prospered and benefited in all manner.

The tentacle of corruption has and continues to be present. America, with all its' immigrants Needs to reconcile with Black and Brown folks and all myelinated spirits living in America and abroad. Our people have needed for a very long time...JUSTICE. And due to our needing, We now, as a race of people, Demand restoration.

We demand restitution. We demand to be reconciled. We demand Justice. Simple justice. We demand equality of protection under the law as American citizens yesterday. We are demanding that our human and civil rights be granted to us freely, without cause or prejudice. We demand that our constitutional rights that others receive freely, even at their birth, are honorably administered to people who do not look as a European.

Again, we are tired of being tired. Our people are tired of being subjugated by white folks in all manners of our existence. We seek not a war with you. We seek not another civil war. We seek not a race war. Even though collectively, Europeans and others have done the most vile, despicable, inconceivable inhumane acts upon our people that would justify and warrant a race war. We seek not to be part of nor engage in resemblance of actively in preparing for such a catastrophic event that shall surely magnify loss of life on both sides of the spectrum. But giving all the circumstances before Man and Mankind, it does appear to be just over the horizon. Unfortunately, for many of us, it feels imminent.

America is a nation of pretense. A nation of make believe. Due to the Caucasoid institutional access (again in all manner), they that sit in high places, who create laws and policies has made it crystal clear that they are adamantly against discussing the word / term "Reparations "with myelinated people living in America and abroad. The Europeans feel no obligation to make amends for the past misdeeds of their ancestors, even though that which happened in the past affects All citizens presently living in America every day of our collective lives. "Speak Truth to Power "…

If in fact the word "Reparations "offends you Europeans and others who look and think as you do - then choose another word that does not offend you. Words such as: CONPENSATION, ATONE, EXPIATE, RECONCILE, MAKE AMENDS, REDEEM, MEND, MAKE UP FOR, REPAY, SETTLE or RECOMPENSE. Pick one that suits you that does not offend you. Choose whatever term that will allow you, the U. S. Government and your co – conspirators to begin the long awaited, overdue sincere negotiations with our assigned representatives. Possibly, you may position yourselves and future generations of your kind to receive Atonement from the Highest of Spirits you may have offended. That really is not my concern.
My concern is for my people.

Words are indeed powerful, yet in and of themselves are useless if not attached to an action, preferably that of Godliness. One's words are meaningless / useless If not attached to exhibiting Humanity upon all beings. If one's word (s) does not produce an action that is reflective in treating all beings as one would like to be treated, then one's words are essentially useless / null and void. If the word (s) that comes out of your mouth is spoken with a forked tongue, you are evil.

Attach a godly action to your words and show an obligatory glimpse towards the administration of Humanity to a people that desperately needs a magnitude of relief from the undeserving unlawful acts, sanctioned by America's governments of all levels.

A racially systemic society and its laws trumps your founding father's constitution and all other historical so-called legal documents. Europeans' laws and policies that are unjust to a people that historically has done white people no wrong are useless to our people in the general scheme of appliance. America has never been considered great through the eyes of the oppressed. But through all of America's Shame, drudgery, and broken dreams, America can officially and genuinely begin to aspire to be great. But only... I say again, only: through Recognizing and Acknowledging TRUTH.

For TRUTH SHALL set All of Man and Mankind FREE from self-hate and the despising of others that are within the minds, bodies, souls, and spirits of human beings living above ground today.

Tomorrow is not promised to any of us living beings. Come forth now with the proper Actions, with the proper attitude and be the change that we all need to be and see.

The time is Now to begin the Healing process that is extremely long overdue for the inhabitants of all living and future generations to come into the bosom of this land we now call America. If All men are created equal, then treat All men equally.

Be about the business of putting a halt to inappropriate behavior by all citizens, especially those who carry weapons of destruction, representing the authority of the law, who are to protect, serve and preserve All life. Acknowledging and make amends by correcting past, present and potential future wrongs of inhumane treatment through the mental illness of racism.

For all of Man and Mankind, the most valuable and precious commodity upon the planet earth is the preservation of ALL HUMAN LIFE. America should not be known to Myelinated beings as the agency of DEATH to America's own legal citizens.

Change America's racial Dichotomy…By whatever Means Necessary.

ALL MELINATED PEOPLE that agree, say…

--Ase'--

All others can say: Amen / if that suits you…

--"Alafia"--

About The Author

Alfred T. Pyles .....Born May 26,1954, Tampa, Fl. Adopted at a young age by his grandparents, Alfred, and Ollie Pyles. Was raised in Ybor City. Attended public schools in Hillsborough, county. All of which were considered predominant black schools, until my senior year of high school, when and where forced integration reared its ugly head.

Sports

While attending Booker T. Washington junior high school, during my 9th grade year (1968-1969), the school resurrected their football team. Our inaugural coach was Louis Jones (Texas Southern). Coach Jones appointed me the team's quarterback. BTW's first football team for many years went undefeated.

Next stop was Middleton high school. There, while in the 10th grade, (1969 – 70), I played on an undefeated JV football team, coached by Aurthur Mays. Coach Mays placed me at the position of running back. Coach Mays also coached his 10th graders to an undefeated JV basketball season, of which we average close to 100 points a game. I played a guard position. I was also voted one of two captains.

I, as a junior, playing on the varsity football team (running back), coached by legendary baseball coach Billy Reed, (who had gone winless the previous year, which was his first full season as head varsity football coach), remarkably, he coached us to an undefeated football season (one tie). One of the greatest feats ever recorded in Tampa, Florida.

During the spring football practices, I was voted captain by my teammates for the upcoming season, which would have been our senior year.

That prestigious honor never unfolded due to the closing of both black high schools.

The school system unceremoniously shut down the only two historical black high schools in the city of Tampa, Hillsborough, county. The two were Blake and Middleton High schools. I would have graduated from Middleton.

I was forced to be bused to a white school, Leto Comprehensive High School. There, again, I was bestowed the honor of being named captain of the varsity football team. There, I tasted defeat for the first time on 3 or 4 occasions, I do not remember exactly. From 9th grade through the 11th grade, I did not lose a game of football, and probably would not have my senior year.

After the season, I won many awards. But this one award that I won distinguishes me from all the others. They who were in charge voted me as becoming the first African American recipient of their prestigious Guy Toph award. Said to be the equivalent (on the high school level, here in Hillsborough County) as the collegiate Heisman Trophy. An honor that I shall forever be recognized as being the First.

That summer, I was voted to play in the North vs South High School All-Star game played at the University of

Florida's football stadium. Today it is the Georgia -Florida high school game.

In that game, which the south won, (I played on the south team), I was fortunate to be voted MVP (1972).

I did not earn a football scholarship to any college or university. But I was given an opportunity by Florida A and M University's newly hired Head football coach, Big Jim Williams (from Tampa's Blake high school).
I departed A and M before the school year was over, due to the birth of my son.

Careers

I enlisted in the Army. I served my country for 4 years, (1973-1977) on active duty. I received an Honorable Discharge.

After basic and Advanced Individual Training (AIT training), my orders were assigned to Ft. Hood, Texas, where I spent most of my military time.

After I was discharged, after working several menial jobs around Killeen, TX, I attempted to pursue my education, and revise my football abilities by enrolling at SW Texas State University, San Marcos, Tx. (President L.B. Johnson's alma mater). Early on in my training and conditioning, I unfortunately pulled a hamstring muscle which halted my progression.

After several semesters, I left school and migrated to Austin, TX. I landed a job working at a Juvenile Residential Treatment Center. From there I received employment at the Travis, County Jail house as a correctional officer. After several years or so, I decided to return to Tampa (1981). In the following 6 years, I worked at then: W.T. Edwards Juvenile Detention Center, USF Bookstore, The Tampa V.A., and as a Federal Correction Officer, in South Miami.

In 1987, an elder working for UPS as a delivery driver, who remembered me from my time at Middleton high school, referred me to UPS's HR department. I was hired. I began my career working part-time at UPS in the warehouse for the first two and a half years. In 1990, I earned full time status working as a Full-time delivery driver until approximately 2007. Still as a full timer, I returned to the hub working as a 22-3 combo worker, working 4 hrs. in the hub, and 4 hrs. as a car washer. My back had begun giving me some problems while as a delivery driver. During the latter part of 2013, my back finally gave out. I was physically unable to do the work that was required of me. I officially retired from UPS in January of 2014, after 25 + years of service.

After a period of inactivity, through a friend, I secured a transporter job working for Eckerd, transporting youth from their residence to the facility where they were schooled, mentored, and preparing for gainful employment.

In May of 2016, I applied for and obtained employment with Enterprise Holdings as a part-time driver near the

Tampa airport. April of 2021, I had a relapse concerning my back issues.

Once rejuvenated, I did not return to Enterprise. In May 2023, through a childhood friend's recommendation, I applied for and obtained employment at a confinement facility for girls, with the job title of Master Control operator, where I am still employed.

Other tidbits: May 2024, I will turn 70 years young.
      Been married twice, divorced twice. No kids from
          either marriage.
      I do have two adult offsprings.
      Presently single.

Raised as a Baptist, I no longer am affiliated.

The only affiliation that I do have is with Olori Temple who prescribes to the Orishas: Selected Heads of the Ifa Religion … The Yoruba Gods and Goddess.

--*Ase'*--